To Bob Pardow

With my warmest
wishes!
Jack R Blam

A PRIVATE'S DIARY

THE BATTLE OF GERMANY AS SEEN THROUGH THE EYES OF AN 18 YEAR OLD INFANTRY RIFLEMAN

Jack R. Blann

JACK R. BLANN

J&L Publishing
Houston

Acknowledgments

I am deeply grateful to my father, R. A. Blann, who insisted that I record my wartime experiences on paper immediately after they happened. Without his urging, the diary, which is the basis of this book, would never have been written. More recently, the assistance of my daughter, Mary Cooper, who placed the original diary onto a word processor, was most helpful in giving me a place to start.

I also want to acknowledge the assistance provided during the preparation of the manuscript by former members of E Company. Harry Kenny has provided much assistance with places and names and has provided several of the photographs used in this text. His remembrance of the battle in the turnip patch gave both of us several laughs and his personal reflections on members of the unit have given me many insights into the people I fought with. W. H. "Hamp" Ward has also assisted with photographs and individual names and provided further information on several of the incidents that I recorded. W. E. "Bill" Roberson supplied details on the early fighting at Remagen that were most helpful to me in understanding some of my notes. W. H. "Bill" Moody, former First Sergeant of E Company, was very helpful in supplying information regarding names of E Company people. I feel a great sadness that Bill did not live to see this mission completed.

Charles McLhinney, brother of PFC. Walter McLhinney who was killed at Oberkirchen, was very helpful in supplying information and pictures regarding his brother. Charlie identified his brother as the radioman killed by the panzer faust at Oberkirchen. At the time of the fighting I knew his brother by sight as Capt. Petty's radioman, but I did not know his name.

I must also acknowledge a debt of long standing to John Henry Pittman, a former colleague at Exxon, who first read the diary in 1953 and urged that I publish it. After many years, I saw John again in 1991 and the first thing that he asked me was "Have you published your diary?". This gave me the final inspiration to begin working on it again.

Jack R. Blann
Colonel, Retired, US Army Reserve
Houston, Texas
January 1997

A Private's Diary

Contents

Contents (Continued)

List of Maps

Prologue

I wrote the original version of this account of my wartime experiences shortly after the fighting ended in Europe in May of 1945. Censorship in Europe ended on May 22nd and my family was anxious to hear about my experiences during the fighting. I hit upon the idea of putting it all down in chronological order and mailing it to my father, one chapter at a time. With the help of some of the others in the 2nd Platoon, I had earlier put together an outline showing the places where our company had been on each day during the fighting in Germany. Several of us mailed those outlines home, but they contained little information other than places and dates. All of us in E Company had discussed each experience so many times that we thought that it was etched indelibly in our minds. Looking back, I see how wrong we were. Many of the events that I wrote about in my diary, I can no longer recall. Others, I recall differently from the way that I described them in the diary. The diary has forever been a reference that does not change with time. Remembering that it was written before any history or summary of the war was published, I am continually amazed at how accurately it compares with official records, where they exist. I typed only one copy of the diary and mailed it each day to my father[1]. I kept no copy for myself; but fortunately, all of the chapters were received and kept by my father until my return home. The original is still stored in my safe at home.

I was only 18 years old when the war in Europe ended. So this account of the war is from the perspective of a very young soldier, thrust suddenly into the experience of a lifetime. I was writing to my father, who was a linotypist for a small daily newspaper in Marlin, Texas. I knew that my father was intimately familiar with every Associated Press dispatch of the war; so, sometimes I did not go into as much detail in explaining some events as I would have for a more

---

[1] R. A. Blann of Marlin, Texas

general audience. I have edited the original version and tried to remove most of the typos. I have also added some detail and additional explanation to the original accounts. I have gone back to the original letters that I wrote home to establish some of the dates and to develop some of the personal information. Unfortunately, because of censorship, my letters home contained some rather standard phrases, such as, "I have been pretty busy lately and haven't been able to write." Translated, this meant that we had been fighting very hard or moving very fast. There was never a hint in any of the letters that I was fighting. I don't think most of us would have wanted our loved ones to know what was happening, even if we could have told them. I have read somewhere that General George Patton wrote his wife every night and gave her a detailed account of everything that transpired during the day. I suppose that Patton could get a letter like that passed through the censors. However, there was no way that an infantry private could bypass censors; so, we didn't even try. After all, the censor was usually the officer in charge of the platoon. He would not have tolerated such foolishness. After censorship ended, it was a different matter. We wanted to tell our story to anyone that would listen. I have tried to leave this account, as much as possible, in the words of the eighteen year old soldier that wrote it.

When the war began in Europe in September of 1939, I was only 13 years old and had not entered High School. I am sure that the last thing that entered my mother's mind was the fact that her oldest son might have to fight in this war. Even before the war began, I had an inordinate interest in it for one so young. But then our teachers at school saw to that, marching us to the music room to hear the speeches of Hitler, Chamberlain, and Roosevelt. During the dark days of August, I stayed glued to the radio listening to H. V. Kaltenborn, Edward R. Murrow, and others trying to forecast what was about to happen. We all knew that the war could start at anytime and on the day the war actually began, I was up before daylight to hear of the German invasion of Poland. Since most events happening in Europe at that time, occurred after *The Waco*

Tribune, our morning paper, went to press, it was difficult to follow the events quickly in the newspaper. In later months, I finally persuaded my father to also subscribe to the *Dallas Morning News.* It had a later deadline and usually contained at least a brief account of the German invasion of Norway and later, the sweep through the Low Countries and France.

In spite of my great interest, I completely missed the bombing of Pearl Harbor, which I regret to this day. I was off playing touch football with a group of friends on that Sunday afternoon and I did not hear of the bombing until I went home at dark. I have never understood why my father, knowing of my interest in the war, did not come and tell me. I can only surmise that the shock of the event kept him glued to the radio.

During my senior year at Marlin High School, I developed a strong attachment to a young lady named Lavonne Fischer, who was later to become my wife. Most of my actions after this time were strongly influenced by the fact that I wanted to remain as near to her as possible. It was at this time that I took the examinations for a military scholarship, and was successful in winning an ASTP (Army Specialized Training Program) Scholarship in Engineering. These scholarships were supposed to allow you to study toward a degree in Engineering at government expense. I was ordered to report to Dallas in July of 1943, where I took my induction physical and was sworn into the Army Enlisted Reserve. I had my heart set on attending Texas A&M and, sure enough, in August I was ordered to report to College Station, Texas for assignment. However, after reaching College Station, and discovering that I was to be sent to a school outside of Texas and far from home, I had second thoughts about the Army scholarship. I asked the Colonel at the station if I had to report as ordered. He asked me how old I was and I said 17. He said, "Son, as long as you are just 17 years old, you don't have to do anything". So I declined the scholarship, and entered Texas A&M in September. During the Christmas recess, I gave Lavonne a ring and asked her to marry me some day in the future when we had control of our lives.

On May 29, 1944, the day after my 18th birthday, I was ordered to report to Camp Wolters, Texas for induction into the army. I was fortunate to remain in Camp Wolters for my Basic Infantry Training since it was only a little over 100 miles from my home. That summer was a real killer for so many of the men from outside of Texas. At least 16 died from the heat and the situation got so bad that the Army began to panic. They took very strong measures to fight the heat exhaustion. Almost every step they took was just the opposite from what would have really helped. They started putting salt in our drinking water and required us to put salt in our canteens. This meant of course that we drank less water, which was the worse thing that we could have done. They would not let us have cool drinks in the mess hall for lunch, but they required, instead, that we drink hot coffee. I wonder how many lives would have been saved by doing what we Texans had been doing all our lives, drinking plenty of cold drinks and water.

I survived Camp Wolters and completed Basic Training with a primary MOS of 'Heavy Weapons Man" [2] in late September of 1944. Everyone in our training battalion over the age of 18 received orders to report to the Pacific Theater of Operations. Those of us who were still 18 years old were sent to Advanced Infantry Training with the 125th Infantry Regiment, first at Camp Maxey, Texas, and later at Camp Gruber, Oklahoma.

---

[2] *Heavy Weapons* in the infantry referred to the 81mm mortar and Heavy 30 caliber water cooled Machine gun. Each infantry battalion was made up of 3 rifle companies and 1 heavy weapons company. The heavy weapons company contained 2 mortar platoons, each consisting of 2 squads of 81mm mortars and 2 machine gun platoons each having of 2 squads of 30cal. heavy machine guns. Each Rifle company also had a weapons platoon consisting of 3 squads of 60mm mortars and 3 squads of 30cal light air cooled machine guns.

That winter in north Texas and Oklahoma did much to prepare us for our forthcoming experiences in Europe. It was bitterly cold in November and December and there was snow and ice on the ground most of the time. We left before daylight every morning, and marched several miles in the slush to train on elaborate training fields with live ammunition and under live fire at all times. We were not properly clothed for the winter, and I couldn't help but wonder how the boys in Europe could survive such cold as they were facing. During the training exercises we had many people seriously wounded and I did not escape injury myself. Only a couple of days before Christmas during a training exercise with booby traps, I stuck my hand into a hole in order to disarm one of the traps. I contacted the triggering mechanism, and when I did, the bomb exploded shredding the fingers on my right hand. The pain was intense and I was rushed by ambulance to the hospital. Although it couldn't have been more than 2 or 3 miles to the hospital, I thought we would never get there. I must have been very pale when I reached the hospital because the doctors were very concerned that I might go into shock. After some morphine, the pain subsided and then I began to worry if I would be able to go home for Christmas. The medics put a large wrapping on my hand and put it in a sling. They told me that they saw no reason why I couldn't go home since there were plenty of Army Hospitals near Marlin. I could check into one of them if my hand started bothering me. I managed to get to Muskogee somehow the next night in order to buy Lavonne a Christmas Gift. The ladies at the department store were very helpful in picking it out since I was almost helpless with my right hand in a sling and still in considerable pain.

Christmas day fell on Monday in 1944, so we were given Class A passes for Sunday and Monday. Those of us from Texas had our hearts set on going home for the holidays. I was very fortunate because there was a passenger train that left Muskogee on Saturday night and went straight to Waco. The train was a madhouse with soldiers standing everywhere. But being a wounded soldier with my hand in a sling, even the young ladies got up and made a seat for me.

Christmas of 1945 was one of the darkest Christmases our country had ever faced. Most families had men in military service fighting overseas. In addition, the battle of the bulge was raging and no one knew at that time where the German offensive would stop. It seemed like ages since those bright days of summer when the Allied armies were racing unchecked across France and it seemed that the war in Europe might end at anytime. Everyone was asking how this could have happened. It was an especially dark time for me since I knew that it would be the last time that I would see Lavonne and my family before I shipped overseas. In addition, I was still recovering from my injury and not able to completely enjoy the time that I had left. Lavonne was working at the telephone company. She managed to get a shift on Christmas Day that allowed her time off in the late afternoon so that she could go with my father and mother as they drove me back to Dallas to catch the train to Muskogee (the Dallas Train left much later than the Waco train so it gave me a few more hours at home). We could travel only 35 miles per hour under the wartime regulations, so it took us over 3 hours to reach Dallas. My father was traveling on old re-treaded tires and we knew that we might have a flat at any minute. However, we made it to Dallas with no problems, although Lavonne told me later that dad's car had two blowouts on the way back to Marlin.

The train at Dallas was not quite as crowded as the earlier train from Muskogee to Waco. I bought a late newspaper but still could find no good news about the fighting in Belgium[3]. I wondered to myself, as I sat on the train' whether I would ever again see a Christmas as bad as this one. Indeed, it was a very bleak journey back to Camp Gruber.

We had our final long bivouac and exercise the first week of the new year. I had managed to miss a few of the bivouacs because of my

---

[3] During the war, many big city newspapers updated their editions every two or three hours so that you could keep up with the latest dispatches from the front.

hand but I was sufficiently recovered to make the final one. We had been told that there would be no more passes and that we were shipping out as soon as we returned from bivouac. Because of the extremely heavy casualties in Europe during the fall and winter of 1944, Congress had amended the Selective Service Act so that 18 year old soldiers could be sent into combat. We were all going to Europe as infantry replacements.

When we got back to the barracks at about noon on Saturday, the first sergeant told us that we would be busy all weekend checking our records and our equipment and that no one could leave the company area. An announcement then came over the call box that I should report to the orderly room. When I got there, I was completely flabbergasted to see Lavonne and her mother along with my mother and my little sister Jane. I was filthy from several days in the field and suffering from lack of sleep; so I had very little patience when I spoke to them. Rather than greeting them joyously, I told them that they had been crazy to come all that way to see me since I would be restricted all weekend. Lavonne had a sheepish grin on her face and she said, "No you won't, we have already talked to the company commander and he has given you a weekend pass. You don't have to be back until Monday morning." They had also already arranged for a hotel room in Muskogee; so, I argued no more and we spent a wonderful weekend saying good-by. On Monday morning I walked the little group to the train and we said a long farewell. I knew this was it, there would be no more good-byes for a long, long time. I had been deeply blessed in having this last chance to visit with my loved ones. I will forever be grateful to Lavonne and her mother for not taking my no for an answer and for facing the hardships and uncertainty of wartime travel, so that we could have these last few hours together. I took the bus back to Gruber and the next day, I joined a lively bunch of mostly 18 year old soldiers as they left by train for New York and the ship that would take them to the fighting front in Europe.

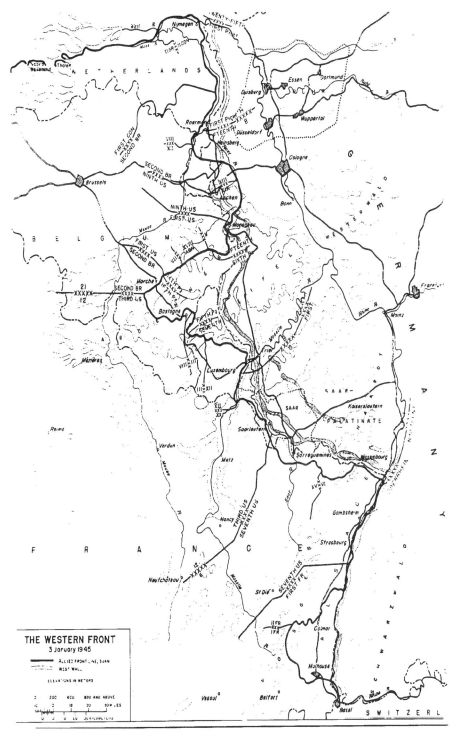

Map 1- The Western Front at the Beginning of 1945

A Private's Diary
Chapter 1

Germany
(Early February 1945)

It was cold and damp as we mounted the open 2 1/2 ton trucks and left Verviers that Sunday morning in early February of 1945. The mist was so thick that we could see very little of the gently rolling Belgian countryside that spread around us. We had all been told a few minutes before that we were being assigned to the 9th Infantry Division of the First Army. Now we were headed for a forward replacement battalion to complete the assignment. None of us had ever heard of the 9th Infantry Division and we were anxious to find out a little more about this unit. I was sorry to that we were leaving Verviers. I had become quite attached to this nice little Belgian town where we had spent the past week, and I had no way of knowing whether I would ever see it again. As it turned out, I saw it again in less than a month.

We were loaded down with a barracks bag and sleeping roll and had also been given a bandoleer of ammunition to throw around our neck. Up until this moment, the war had always been somewhere off in the distant future. We all knew that we would get there some day, but that day was a long way down the road. Now, the future had arrived, and the war was getting closer by the minute. In Verviers we had heard the far off rumble of artillery and at night had gone up on a hill near our billets to see the flash of guns firing in the distance. But even then, the quaint, peaceful, nature of Verviers had cloaked the nearness of battle.

It was hard to realize that less than a month ago we had all been training in the hills along the Arkansas River of Oklahoma. It all seemed so far away and long ago. We had not spent much time in transit coming over. There were a few days spent in Fort Meade and

Camp Kilmer getting everything ready for the trip overseas. From Ft. Meade, Maryland I had managed to get into Washington, D. C. for a visit; the first time that I had seen the nations capital. Everything had been covered in a blanket of snow and it was bitterly cold. I had had a chance to go to the inauguration of President Roosevelt for his fourth term, but the weather was just too bad. Very few people attended and those that went said that the President looked very old and sick. Standing outside to take the oath in such weather certainly didn't help his health. From Ft. Meade we moved on to Camp Kilmer at New Brunswick, New Jersey for our final embarkation orders. At Camp Kilmer, we literally had a ball, visiting New York City every day. What a town for servicemen; there were free tickets to the Broadway shows, radio broadcasts, and all types of sporting events.[4] But best of all was the Stagedoor Canteen, where every serviceman was treated like a hero. Nearly all of the servicemen visiting New York were headed overseas and it seemed that America, at this time with the 'Battle of the Bulge" still raging, could not do enough to show its appreciation to those of us going into battle.[5]

---

[4] The USO dispensed free tickets every afternoon at 4 PM and you could take your choice of the shows and events that were available. I managed to see *One Touch of Venus, Mexican Hayride, Bloomer Girl,* and the latest *Olsen & Johnson revue* along with *Sonja Heine and her Ice show* at Madison Square Garden. At CBS, I watched "The Henry Aldrich Show" being broadcast to west coast audiences. All the radio broadcasts were live in those days, so the same show had to be repeated for the audiences in the different time zones. In the middle of Times Square there was a building that dispensed refreshments and radio tickets. I think it was sponsored by one of the cigarette companies. At least there was always a lot of show tickets for *Perry Como and the Chesterfield Hour* that was broadcast every day at 6 PM. You could also make recordings at this facility to mail home. These were actual cardboard phonograph records, since tape recorders were yet to be invented.

[5] The Stagedoor Canteen was sponsored by the Theater Guild of New York and different members of the guild entertained the troops each day. There were always charming ladies there who made it a point to single out each soldier and talk to him as long he desired. The casts of the Broadway shows also entertained each day. I remember seeing the cast of *Carmen Jones* present numbers from that show, which was very popular at the time.

The snow was deep in the city and it was still bitterly cold. The ladies at the Stagedoor Canteen could not understand why I did not wear an overcoat. Being from Texas, wearing an overcoat had never entered my mind. I actually had more problems with heat than cold. The Broadway theaters were warm and the wool clothing that I wore had been impregnated with a chemical to make then impervious to poison gas. The combination of warmth and chemical caused me to itch and scratch something fierce while I sat and watched the shows. Bertrand, the kid who slept in the bunk next to mine, was from New Orleans and had never before seen snow. One of the fellows who lived on Long Island took him to his home to meet his family and while they were there, they went for a horse drawn sleigh ride. Bertrand was ecstatic when he told me about it the next day.

Finally, we took a ferry across the Hudson River from Jersey City to the pier where the troopship was docked. An army band played *Over There* and many of the other old standard war songs as we boarded the troopship. As usual, the Red Cross was there and they gave each of us a little cloth bag stuffed with toilet articles and other little gifts. The ship was the *USS Wakefield*, which, before the war had been named the *Manhattan*, and had been one of the fast ocean liners that regularly traveled between the United States and Europe. I was seasick most of the way across the extremely rough North Atlantic, but still managed to work in a detail that moved Post Exchange supplies from the hole of the ship to the ships stores. We crossed the wintry North Atlantic without escort in 5 days, landing early on the sixth day in Liverpool, England. Immediately we boarded a troop train for Southampton. Once again the Red Cross girls were there. On the train they passed out coffee and doughnuts and we all mistook them for American girls. But they laughed and said no, they were English. In Southampton, we stood on the docks where the Red Cross once again served us coffee and doughnuts. We were told to eat all we wanted because we would get no more food that night. Then we boarded an LST headed for Le Havre, France.

The LST was just a big hollow hull that been used to disembark tanks on the beaches during the invasion. It was fitted out with litters along the side so that during the invasion, it could evacuate the wounded on the return trip. We were allowed to use the litters for sleeping, but there wasn't much sleep that night. Some one kept setting off depth charges all the way across the channel. Each time, the charge exploded, the big open LST would vibrate like a drum. The Port of Le Havre was still not useable, so they pulled the nose of the LST up onto the beach and, after a dozer pushed sand up to the ramp, we walked onto the beach with dry feet.

France was a sight to behold, even in wartime. Everything reminded of the movies we had seen of doughboys in France during World War I. But nothing had prepared us for the open toilets in the train stations, the prostitutes on every corner, and the army PRO[6] stations in every block. After a night in a tent, we marched early in the morning to the train station where, once again, an Army band serenaded us as we boarded the same old forty and eight box cars (forty men or eight horses)[7] that many of our fathers and uncles had ridden in World War I. The cars were very small and we were packed in them with hardly enough room to sit. This was our home for two days as we traveled toward Verviers. Of course, as the train crawled slowly across France, we had know idea where we were going. There was continued speculation as we passed through countless small towns in northern France, none of which we had ever heard of before. There was also an awful lot of praying that was done on that train. Suddenly, high spirited young kids were deadly serious. The first night, one of the fellows led the whole car in reciting *The Lord's Prayer*.

It took two days of stopping and starting to reach Verviers. There was an army kitchen on the train, so twice each day the

---

[6] PRO stood for prophylactic and at these stations army medics passed out various material for the prevention of venereal disease.
[7] The cars actually had their capacity - 40 men and 8 horses (40 Hommes - 8 Cheveux) - stenciled on the side in French.

kitchen had to be unloaded and set up, the meals cooked, and the troops fed. This took several hours of time for each meal. Sometimes the train moved only a short distance before it stopped again for the next meal. Just before we reached Verviers, we passed through Liege, Belgium, and we thought at first that this might be our destination. Near the railroad track there was a huge crater caused by a recent German buzz bomb.[8] Only a few mile further on was Verviers. What a relief to reach the relative quiet and peace of this beautiful little city.

The time in Verviers had really flown. We were issued and test fired our rifles along with being treated to the other necessities for fighting a war. Now we were on our way to the front and on the last leg of a very long trip. After traveling a few miles out of Verviers, we came to a crossroads where one sign marked "Aachen" pointed to the right and another labeled 'Liege" pointed left. We turned to the right and kept on moving down the foggy road. Just a few miles further down this road, we came to a small village. On the outskirts of the village there was a little sign in English with the one word, "Germany", written on it. The sign sent a shock through all of us. Now we were actually in Germany and moving toward what must be the front line. Along the road, we began to pass more and more tanks and armor parked along the shoulders and in the muddy fields adjacent to the roads.

A few miles across the German border, we entered the Hurtgen Forest. already famous for the intense fighting that went on there during October and November of 1945. Here we saw the first section of Hitler's renowned *West Wall*, better known as the *Seigfried Line*. As we entered the fortifications, we passed blasted concrete pillboxes that had been destroyed months earlier, when the allies first entered Germany. Then, we crossed the first row of dragon teeth. These so called dragon teeth were huge concrete

---

[8] The original German V-1 rockets made a distinctive putt putt or buzzing noise like a high speed motor, hence the name *buzz bomb*.

pillars used to stop tanks. At one time they had been one of the most visible parts of the Seigfried line, which stretched along the German border from Belgium to Switzerland. We were puzzled by the fact that the road went right straight through the obstacles. To us, this seemed to defeat the purpose of the fortifications.

Almost immediately, we entered the old German city of Aachen. In the 12th Century, Aachen had been the capital of Charlemagne and seat of the Holy Roman Empire. It had been completely destroyed during the house-to-house fighting in October of 1944[9]. There was not a building in the central part of the city that was not in ruins. We traveled down large boulevards with ruins piled high on each side, but our trucks didn't even slow down in Aachen. After leaving the town, we traveled almost due south. The roads gradually got worse and worse until they became a quagmire. There were engineer units all along these roads trying to lay logs as a base for the vehicles to drive upon, but there didn't seem to be enough logs to lay everywhere.

The next town that we came to was the little mountain town of Monschau. Monschau is located on a little swift flowing stream in the Eifel Mountains. The stream is, in fact, the upper reaches of the Roer River. We didn't go down into the town, but skirted around it and went back to the west a few kilometers almost to the Belgian border to a little country village called Kalterherberg. This village had been heavily fought over during the "Battle of the Bulge". Now, there was hardly a house left standing. We were later to find out that many men of the 9th Division had many bitter experiences in and around Kalterherberg during that period.

We were assigned to tents and in the distance we could hear our big guns firing steadily. At this time, we were told that the front line on the Roer River was about seven miles away. There were

---

[9] Aachen was captured by the "Big Red One" , the First Infantry Division (See " Bloody Aachen" by Charles Whiting, Lee Cooper, London, 1976 for a complete account of the battle of Aachen.)

dead cattle and horses laying everywhere in the fields around Kalterherberg, bloated by the changes in temperature. Even now there was still a good bit of snow along the roads, especially on the higher hills and mountains.

That night there was a chapel service for all religious denominations and not many of our group missed it. We stayed at the replacement depot only over night and left again at eleven the next morning. We went back over the same road by which we had come from Monschau, but this time we went down into the town where the rear echelon of the 9th Division was located. The rear echelon was located in a big textile mill and there was thread still on all the machines and looms in the mill. We threw our sleeping rolls and packs in among the big looms and were cautioned not to touch anything in the building because it all belonged to civilians. It was here in Monschau that we first heard *Bed Check Charlie*. This was a lone plane that flew over just after dark and we all assumed that it was German. It could just as well have been one our own planes since it never fired a shot or dropped a bomb. In the days ahead it became a familiar sound.

There were plenty of German civilians in Monschau, something that we had not seen before in Germany. However, we were not allowed to speak to them. The next day we were assigned to our different regiments and we parted with a lot of our buddies. Bertrand, whose name was next to mine on the shipping roster and who had been a buddy of mine since we had trained together at Camp Gruber, was assigned to a heavy weapons company of a different regiment. All of us had been assigned a heavy weapons MOS (Military Occupational Specialty) after we finished basic training, but since the casualty rate was much higher for infantry riflemen, most of us were now assigned as replacements for the riflemen. I was disappointed at being separated from Bertrand and kidded him some about how lucky he was to get the heavy weapons assignment and not to be going to an infantry line company like the rest of us.

Several others of us who had trained together including Deal, Denny, Myers, and Boyle, were assigned to a company in the 47th Infantry Regiment[10], and after the briefest good-byes, we were on a truck heading for the outfit. The regiment was off down a dirt road that seemed to be nothing but a sea of mud. On the way, we passed guns which were firing towards the front line stretched out along the Roer River. The 47th Infantry Regiment was located around the town of Schmidt, which had been won finally and for good a few days before by the 78th Infantry Division. Schmidt had been captured briefly by the 28th Infantry Division after an extremely bloody fight back in November of 1944 in one of the most famous battles of World War II. The 28th Division had attacked and captured Schmidt along a very narrow road through the very steep Kall River gorge. They were unable to hold the town and a strong German panzer group had quickly recaptured it. Schmidt commanded the high ground in the entire Eifel area and the Germans had been desperate to keep control of it in order to insure the surprise of their attack in the Ardennes, which we called the "Battle of the Bulge".

I thought that my joining the fighting on the Western Front at Schmidt was the strangest coincidence. While I had been training in

---

[10]An infantry division consisted of 3 regiments of infantry, an artillery group, and numerous service battalions and companies such as medical, engineer, signal, ordnance, quartermaster, military police and reconnaissance. The 3 infantry regiments that made up the 9th Division were the 60th Infantry, 39th Infantry and the 47th Infantry. Each infantry regiment consisted of 3 battalions of infantry. Each battalion of infantry contained 3 rifle companies and 1 heavy weapons company. The companies of each regiment were designated alphabetically beginning with A, B, C, and D companies which were assigned to the 1st Battalion. E, F, G, and H companies were assigned to the 2nd Battalion and I, K, L, and M Companies were assigned to the 3rd Battalion. For some reason there were no J Companies. The first 3 companies named in each battalion were the rifle companies and the last company was the heavy weapons company. Each infantry regiment also contained a service company, a cannon company, and an antitank company.

the states back in November, I had read all about the fighting at Schmidt. It was one of the very few battlegrounds in Europe that I could identify by name and had heard of before I left the states. Now, it was a little unnerving to be joining the unit at such a familiar (at least from newspaper accounts) place.

In February of 1945, Schmidt really was not a town. It was just a few completely destroyed houses scattered along a long ridge line. There was little to distinguish between the three small villages of Harscheidt, Kommerscheidt and Schmidt that occupied the ridge line near the road junction. The 3rd Battalion was positioned along the river and holding the front, while the other two battalions were in reserve around regimental headquarters. I was assigned to the 2nd Battalion late in the afternoon. Colonel George W. Smythe[11], the regimental commander, met us first and gave us a brief welcoming talk. I was to find out later that Col. Smythe was already a legendary figure with the men of the 47th because of his exploits in gathering together various scattered units to stop the German attacks during the Battle of the Bulge. Col. Smythe told us that it wouldn't take us long to become combat wise and that this was the only way to survive in combat. He gave an example of an incident that had happened between him and his sergeant only a few days before. He said that he was crossing a snowy field with the sergeant trailing along behind when he turned around to say something to the sergeant. It was then that he noticed that the sergeant was stepping along in his footprints trying to make sure that if there were any mines in the field, the Colonel would have already found them. Col. Smythe said, 'that's what I mean by being combat wise, its the little things that may make the difference". A few weeks later, the colonel was promoted to brigadier general and left the division.

---

[11] Colonel George W. Smythe had been an All-American halfback in the class of 1924 at West Point. He had joined the 47th in Africa just after the fighting in Tunisia and had led the 47th through Sicily, France and Belgium. His exploits in leading the regiment during the Battle of the Bulge had won him the Distinguished Service Cross.

After Colonel Smythe's colorful talk, we strolled through the mud over to 2nd Battalion headquarters, which was located on another hill. There, after Lt. Col. Lewis E. "Chip" Maness, the battalion commander, gave us another talk, we went to join our companies. I was assigned to E Company where Captain Frank Petty was Company Commander and Lt. Harry Kenny was his executive officer. Lt. Jay Garner was one of the platoon leaders in Company E, but the 2nd Platoon, to which I was assigned, had no platoon leader at that time. It was my understanding that the former platoon leader of the 2nd Platoon had been moved over to F Company to command a *5th Platoon* of black soldiers that had just been attached to F Company. So far as I know, this was the first time in Europe that black soldiers had been mixed in with white soldiers in the infantry companies. The 5th platoon was still training back in France and had not joined the unit at that time.

Company E[12] was dug in on the north side of a long ridge which overlooked the little town of Kommerscheidt. When we got to the company, the fellows were just eating chow, and we dropped our equipment and joined in the chow line. The unit members were all very friendly and tried to make us feel at home. They told us that they were living in some holes over on the side of a hill. I was assigned to the 2nd Platoon but there wasn't any place for me to stay that night in the holes on the hill; so, I stayed in part of an old barn with some of the mortar section of the 4th Platoon. I unrolled my sleeping bag and started to take off my boots before crawling into the bag. One of the mortar men saw me and told me that it wasn't wise to take your boots off while you slept, since you might have to leave in a hurry. I put my boots back on and slept with them on that night and for many nights thereafter.

---

[12]An infantry rifle company had an assigned strength of 193 men. These were divided into 3 rifle platoons and a weapons platoon. Each of the rifle platoons had 3 squads of 12 men when they were at full strength.

The next day I turned in my heavy roll to the company supply[13] and kept only a pack of my most essential articles. Sergeant Ward was squad leader of the 2nd Platoon, so after breakfast I went out to his hole and he took me over and introduced me to the other fellows in the squad. I was put in the same hole with Jenkins, Hart, and Roberson. Roberson was a buck sergeant and our assistant squad leader.

The hole had been dug into the side of the hill. On the lower side, sand bags had been stacked to complete the four walls. There was a little straw on the floor to sleep on and the roof was made of old doors. The roof leaked when it rained, but it stopped raining that day and the sun began to shine. We felt relatively safe from artillery in this hole since we were on the reverse slope of the hill.

One of the first sights that all of the newcomers were taken to see at Schmidt was the bodies of the dead Jerries[14] on top of the hill just a few yards above our holes. There were quite a few bodies scattered around on the hill and they had been there for some time. They had been looted many times already and their pockets were turned inside out. On the hill, there was a long slit trench which the Germans had used as part of their defense of the town; but it was now being used as a garbage dump. Some of the fellows were afraid to go up on the

---

[13]It was customary to send a complete duffel bag of equipment to the front with each replacement. These were then turned into the supply section and reissued as required. This was a highly successful way that the army found for moving supplies up to the front.

[14] We called the Germans many different names during the fighting. The term *Jerries* was probably one of the nicer names that had probably originated with the English. There was nothing derogatory about the term *Jerries*, as far as I know. The most common name that we used during the actual fighting, and it was certainly meant to be derogatory, was the term *Kraut* or *Krauts* to describe the enemy. I don't think that I ever heard the Germans referred to at the front by the term *Nazis*, which was so common in the newspapers and unit histories of the time. Their leadership might have been *Nazis* but we never believed that these people we were fighting were anything but common soldiers like ourselves.

hill at night in fear of falling into one of the trenches with the dead Germans. I was told that during the first night at Schmidt, some of the unit used the trenches for protection. However, even then, some of the men would not stay in the German trenches and preferred to sleep exposed on the ground beside them.

Chapter 2

Schmidt
(From about February 20-28)

The armies along the Western Front were still maneuvering into position for the big push to the Rhine. General Patton was still cleaning up remnants of the German Ardennes Offensive along the German-Belgian border to the south. None of this was apparent to those of us waiting in Schmidt and along the Roer River. We stayed in Schmidt for quite sometime and all we did while we there was lay around and take life easy. Our section of the front was relatively quiet. Unless we looked over the hill toward Nideggen and the Roer River, we could hardly tell that the war was going on. We built a big fire every day and we would sit around it and talk about home and of combat experiences. These experiences of our veteran comrades were eagerly absorbed by all of us new men. We hoped to gain some small measure of intelligence that would give us a little advantage over our enemy when the fighting began again. On their part, the combat veterans wanted to know what was going on back home and about the latest song hit or movie that may be playing back there. I mentioned that *Drinking Rum and Coca Cola*[15] by the Andrews Sisters was the big hit back home, but no one at the front had heard of it so I had to sing a few verses to let everyone know what it sounded like.

Most of the fellows were young, unmarried, men like myself and we talked about girl friends and family and what we would do after the war was over. Myers, one of the men that had come overseas with me and joined the platoon when I did, was not like the rest of us. He was much older and had three children back home. It was difficult

---

[15]During the winter of 1944-45, *Drinking Rum and Coca Cola* was a big hit on the juke boxes and in the record shops back in the states, but, because of its supposedly suggestive lyrics, it had not been broadcast on the radio. Consequently, no one in the European Theater had heard of it.

to understand why fathers as old as Myers had been sent into combat but Myers didn't complain about his situation.

During the time at Schmidt, since several artillery units were located nearby, there was continual artillery fire going out over our head toward the German line. However, only two shells came in from the German side and they hit over across the hills from us. There was always test firing of our weapons and even the mortars were fired into the valley that led down toward the Kall River Gorge. Our favorite target seemed to be a large shellhole beside a road where a dead German was laying. The mortar platoon was always laying shells into this hole.

The old castle at Nideggen, high above the Roer River, was easily visible from our hill. We watched it and exchanged many stories and speculation about what the Germans were doing in the castle. It seemed a little strange to be standing on the hill and looking into the German lines, although the castle was about 3 miles away as the crow flies. Of course the Germans in the castle could see us too. That's why we were dug in on the opposite side of the hill.

Although by now there was not much snow, it was still quite cold so we spent much of the time at Schmidt trying to make our holes more comfortable. We used explosives to try to make the holes in the frozen and rocky hill a little deeper. We also rummaged around through the wrecked houses to find odds and ends to make stoves. One day the stove in our hole set the hay on fire so we had to go out and find some way to keep the fire away from the hay on the floor. We found a piece of metal on which to set the stove and this solved our problem. We also found a piece of pipe to serve as a stove pipe and let the smoke escape from the sleeping area. Pieces of furniture and wood were retrieved from the wrecked houses to burn as firewood. Some of the furniture had been quite beautiful and it seemed a shame to burn it up this way.

Everyone tried to catch up on their letter writing. It was amazing how much we worried about the folks back home. Since we didn't want them to think we were in any danger or to worry about us, most of our letters said little or nothing about the war or how bad the conditions were at the front. For the first time in almost two months, I had a permanent address and the first thing that I did was to let everyone at home know about it. Of course, I had not gotten any mail since I had left Oklahoma, although I had tried to write home every day. I didn't realize it at the time, but it would still be many more weeks before I would have a letter from home. Stationery for writing the letters was not easy to come by in the front lines. Here at Schmidt we were relatively stable and because of this we could get stationery from the mail clerk. V-Mail stationery was always available and supposed to be the fastest way to write. I didn't like it because you could only write a few lines on the page. It was more of a note than a letter. The postal service would photograph the page and send the film back to the states where it would be processed and mailed to the recipient. We could send V-mail and regular mail free. Air mail was actually the fastest way to send a letter, but it required a six-cent airmail stamp and sometimes they were pretty hard to find. All of our mail was censored by one of the unit officers, so we could not say anything about what we were doing or where we were.

At night, we pulled one hour of guard duty apiece. On my second night of guard, I noticed that over in the direction of Cologne a streak of tracers would go up into the night sky every once in a while. It was a beautiful sight to see these red antiaircraft bursts at night. The planes would then drop flares that would light up the countryside. The antiaircraft bursts never came close to us at night, so we imagined that it was the Germans firing at our planes.

On every clear day, we would see hundreds and hundreds of planes[16] come over us to bomb the Germans. They were probably

---

[16]The American Air Force bombed in the daytime and the British bombed at night.

bombing Cologne, although we could not see Cologne from where we were located. We would walk to the top of the hill and watch the bombers operate. As they crossed the German lines you could see the German flak[17] start blossoming all around them. The flak looked just liked like puffs of black smoke, but it would start popping every where. Then you would see one of our planes that always flew in perfect formation go into a dive and never pull out. Finally a great column of black smoke would rise from the ground where it had fallen.

You could see the planes as they circled their target and came back again and again. After awhile, the Germans would send up one or two fighters and then our fighters would start chasing the German fighters like a dog chasing a cat. Every once in awhile, they would chase a plane over us and then our ack-ack would start flying from every direction. I never saw our people hit anything, but they had a lot of fun and shot-up a lot of ammunition. One day, a German jet propelled[18] plane came over at a very slow speed, but no matter how much we shot at it, no one seemed to be able to hit it. It was a strange looking plane without propellers.

Sometimes, we noticed something falling from the planes. We at first thought that someone was bailing out. But we saw it coming from all the planes and then we realized that the planes were dropping something. We found out afterwards that the planes were dropping aluminum or tin foil to confuse the German radar. We later saw this foil covering the ground all over Germany.

---

[17]Common expression used for bursting German antiaircraft fire.
[18]Jet propelled was the term we used at that time for what we now call jets. This was a very new weapon of the Germans and apparently the U. S. Airforce had nothing to counter it.

One day a rumor started around the unit that the Ninth Army[19] had crossed the Roer up north of us and was pushing down the River. We didn't believe the rumor until a day or so later it was confirmed in the *Stars and Stripes*.[20] Every day we would prepare to cross the Roer river, but every night they would call it off, and we would settle down to another nights sleep. We heard all sorts of stories about offers of 30 day furloughs to anyone that would swim the Roer with a rope. However, the water in the river stayed too high and too fast for anyone to successfully cross it.

During the night of the 25th of February, our guns began a terrific artillery barrage all along the front. The ground shook continuously with no let up. No one in the unit had ever heard such an artillery barrage as this before. It continued all of the next day and into the next night. We knew that the units north of us must be crossing the Roer and we felt that it would be only a matter of time before we jumped off to the attack. But still we waited. Then, on the 27th of February it came, the old Calvary command, *saddle up*. This had now become one of the most dreaded orders in the infantry. We were told to be ready to move out to cross the river by ten that night.

---

[19]At the beginning of the spring offensive in February 1945, seven allied armies were present on the western front. They were arrayed along a north-south line, near or just inside the border of Germany, as follows:

> First Canadian on the far north commanded by Lt. Gen. Henry D. G. Crerar,
> Second British commanded by Lt. Gen. Miles C. Dempsey,
> Ninth US commanded by Lt. Gen. Wm. H. Simpson,
> First US Commanded by Lt. Gen. Courtney H. Hodges,
> Third US Commanded by Lt. Gen. George S. Patton
> Seventh US commanded by Lt. Gen. Alexander M. Patch, and
> First French commanded by Gen. John de Lattre de Tassigny, located

on the far south of the line.
The First Canadian and Second British formed an Army Group under Field Marshall Bernard L. Montgomery. The Ninth, First and Third U.S. formed an Army Group under Lt. Gen. Omar Bradley, and the Seventh U.S. and First French formed and Army Group under Lt. Gen. Jacob L. Devers.
[20]The Ninth Army crossed the Roer on February 23rd.

We checked all of our ammo, oiled our rifles, and then just sat there waiting. At ten, an order came down that we wouldn't move till four the next morning so, "go to bed and get some sleep". We threw another log into our makeshift stove made from an old barrel and went to sleep.

We got up at three the next morning to eat our breakfast. We ate without a sign of light, and then went back to our holes to wait. No order to move came, so we spent the next day sleeping and waiting and finally moved out at four in the afternoon. We learned that units to the north of us[21] had crossed the river on assault bridges in the Ninth Army sector and driven south down the Roer, allowing units of the 9th Division (39th Infantry Regiment) to cross on assault bridges that the 1st Division had put across the river. The 9th Division, after it secured the other bank, then put its own bridges across the river. This meant, to our great relief, that our unit would not have to make a frontal assault across the river.

As we moved out, I was loaded down with three extra shells of Bazooka ammo and three bandoleers of rifle ammo along with two hand grenades. I was beginning to sweat before we had gone a hundred yards. The road was still muddy and we passed a little sign tacked on the side of the road saying to keep your distance because of intermittent shelling. The road was up one hill and down another till we came to the Roer River where a Bailey Bridge[22] had been thrown across the river. We crossed the Bailey Bridge and walked on up one of the hills till we were about to drop. In fact, many of the platoon had already fallen out. Hart had dropped out because the heavy BAR (Browning Automatic Rifle)[23] he was carrying was getting to be too much for him. A BAR weighs 22 pounds with clip

---

[21] 1st Infantry Division

[22] The Bailey bridge was a solid truss type structure that had no intermediate support. It could be used to cross relatively narrow streams and was supported at each end by the river bank or an abutment.

[23] The Browning Automatic Rifle weighed 19.4 lb. and carried a 20 round clip. It could be fired rapidly like a machine gun.

compared to the 9 pounds of the M-1 rifle. All along the road, many of the soldiers had discarded their overshoes and anything else that they could do without. Many of the men had what we called the GI's (a chronic form of dysentery) and the climb was especially hard on them. Fortunately, I had not developed the symptoms of this disease at this time.

When we got to the top of the hill, we looked out upon the famous Cologne plain, which the First Army had been trying to reach since September of 1944. There were flat open fields ahead of us, but it was getting dark and we couldn't see very much of the terrain. We continued along this highway until we came to the outskirts of a town. Then we stopped and waited for orders that would tell us what to do next. We must have waited two hours. We lay down on the road until we got too cold and then we stood up and stomped around trying to stay warm. Our clothes were still damp from the sweat of the afternoon march. Because of all the clothes we were wearing, we got very hot and sweaty while we were marching. Then, when we stopped for long, we nearly froze. Some of the fellows smoked cigarettes underneath their panchos. The pancho was an army styled rain coat that looked like a piece of oil cloth with a hole in the middle[24]. You put your head through the hole and the rest of the cloth dropped around your body. We could hear German shells coming in behind us and in the distance there was the sound of all kinds of small arms fire.

When we finally got our orders, we were more than ready to move. We went through the little town of Nideggen and past the old castle that we had observed for so long. In Nideggen, we saw armor parked in between all of the houses and assault 155 mm "long tom"[25] artillery parked along the streets. We talked to some of the

---

[24] The pancho later became famous is Korea and Vietnam but I had never seen one before arriving in Germany.

[25] These were the 155mm GMC M12 self propelled artillery pieces that had been sent to Europe in 1944. It used the M3 medium tank chassis for transport.

fellows and found out that this unit was the 9th Armored Division[26] and that they were pushing off early the next morning to attack toward the Rhine. This was the start of the drive that ended with the capture of the Remagen bridge by a unit of the 9th Armored Division.

We didn't stay in the town, but instead went on out the other end to a big field where there was a long German trench. The battalion bedded down for the night in the trench. It was so dark in the trench, that I had problems locating my rifle when I laid it down. Then when I found it, I didn't know whether it was mine or someone else's. Up until this time, I had always identified my rifle by the serial number. I suddenly realized that in the dark, trying to read the serial number would be useless. One of the other guys said that I should carve some mark on the stock of the rifle so that I would know it was mine as soon as I picked up. The next morning I carved my initials on a particular part of the stock and I had no more problems identifying it after that[27].

We were up bright and early the next morning. We could see down below us a large town which we found out was Duren. The Roer River could be seen twisting along through it. To the east in the distance, we could see the large brick chimneys and the cathedral spires of the city of Cologne. At that time Cologne was about twenty miles in front of us. There was hot chow waiting for us over behind a clump of trees, and as soon as we had finished, we started to move again. Over in a nearby field, we could see a dead GI

---

[26] An armored division was made up of three battalions of infantry (roughly equivalent to one infantry regiment) and three battalions of tanks. All of the infantrymen could be transported on armored half-track carriers. The armored division was specially designed for "highly mobile warfare" and could move very rapidly when properly employed.

[27] After the war, Col. Maness threatened to make me pay for the rifle since I had damaged government property in this way. Never-the-less, I had not impaired the operation of the rifle and I still don't know of a better solution to the problem.

laying with his helmet propped on a rifle so that the boys that pick up the dead[28] could find him. We went on back through town and at this time we had our four tanks and four tank destroyers (TD's) trailing along behind us. These were the platoon of tanks and tank destroyers that were regularly assigned to the battalion for close support.[29] The tanks were medium M4 Sherman tanks that carried a 76 mm gun. The tank destroyers looked very much like the Sherman tanks, but carried a 90 mm gun. You could easily tell the difference in the two by the fact that the tank destroyer had an open top turret, whereas the tank turret was sealed.

---

[28]Grave Registration Units, usually made up of members of the Division Band.
[29]This was the 2nd Platoon, 746th Tank Battalion and the 2nd Platoon of the 899th Tank Destroyer Battalion.

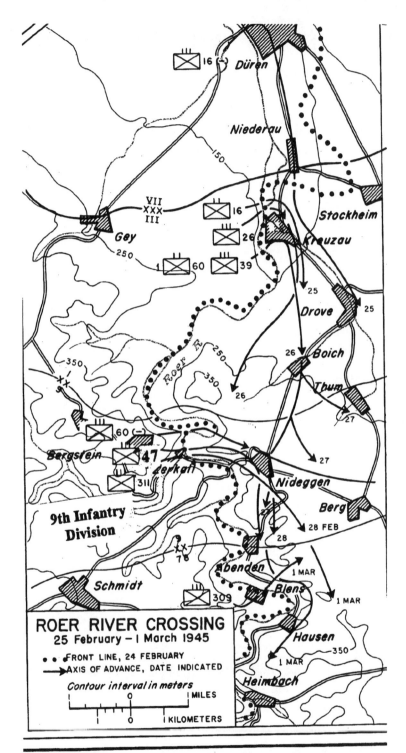

Map 2 - Ninth Infantry Division Roer River Crossing Near Nideggen

38

Chapter 3

Toward Cologne
(March 1)

We moved out of town a little distance directly toward Cologne and soon came to the top of a hill where there were bodies of dead German's laying everywhere. There were two German Mark 5 tanks knocked out over on one side of the hill and there were dead German soldiers laying all around the vehicles. We felt that this action must have occurred the day before, although the vehicles were still smoking. Beside one of the vehicles, we noticed that one of the Germans was still alive, even though he had been blown almost in two and his legs were missing. His eyes were open and he was moaning. There was no way that this man could recover from such wounds. In fact, we couldn't understand how he had managed to live this long. We were all disturbed by the suffering that the man must be enduring, so one of the officers walked over and closed the man's eyes, and shot him in the head with his forty five[30].

From the hill, you could see the battle line still quite some distance in front of us and you could see the bursting artillery in the distance all along the front. The panorama stretching before us reminded me of some of the panoramic drawings of battles that I had seen in *Life Magazine*. The line seemed to bulge out in the direction of Cologne and it looked as if some of our troops must be getting pretty close to the big city. At this time, a big armada of B-26's flew over and began to bomb Cologne and the roads around the city. We were so close to the bombers that we could see the bombs as they left the planes. There was no flack going up against them, probably because the retreat had thrown the antiaircraft defenses into confusion.

---

[30]Unit officers were usually armed with either Colt 45mm pistols or 30 caliber carbines.

Some of the men looked around the dead Germans on the ground around us to see if there were any valuables that might be worth picking up. As for myself, I never became hardened enough that I could loot the dead. I didn't want to have anything to do with the dead soldiers. It was hard enough to just look at these men, killed at such a young age. One good looking young German boy had long black hair that was usually combed straight back from his forehead. Now it had fallen forward over his face. I could see myself lying there.

We left the hill and went down into a little ravine where we waited for our orders. While we were there, chow came up and we had a hot meal. I picked up some old German and French money laying on the ground in the ravine, probably discarded by some of the looters because it apparently had no value. Then it began to sprinkle, and we began huddling around each other to talk about what the future might hold for us. All of us were hoping that maybe we would never catch up with the front lines, but of course, we all knew that sooner or later we would.

At about four o'clock, we began moving down the road through a burning town. There were two American light tanks[31] still burning alongside the road. There were also shell duds that didn't explode laying on and off the road and we were careful not to kick them with our feet. The bodies of dead Germans were laying all along the road and an occasional American jeep would come by with a dead GI laying on it. There were also the bodies of a few GI's laying alongside the roads.

We moved into a thickly wooded area where our tanks were stopped and firing straight ahead. Our mortars were also set up nearby and firing at some target just over the hill. We moved deep into the brush and began digging our holes for the part of the night that we were going to be there. Occasionally we could hear a mine

---

[31]These were probably M5 Stuart tanks used extensively by reconnaissance units

go off after some unlucky vehicle had run over it. By now, my ears were completely accustomed to the sounds of combat and I could identify each and every sound. I could tell the difference between a mine or an artillery shell and I could recognize the sounds of the different types of rifles and machine guns as they were fired. Our lives depended upon quick recognition of sounds and their recognition came almost as second nature to us.

We got our hole dug in the rocky ground by dark and then we stretched a top of tree branches over it as some protection against the cold night. Our supper finally came up to us after dark and Sergeant Ward helped us to find our way back to the road where we could get it. By now this tall, lanky, slow talking Georgia boy had become a father figure to many of us in the squad. He was slightly older than the rest of us and had had considerably more experience and training. We respected him in a way that would be hard to explain to those who had never been in our situation.

We turned in the overshoes that some of us had been carrying all of this the time on our backs. It was still hard finding our way back to our holes after dark; but we finally managed it, and now we were able to crawl into our sleeping bags for some rest.

At about twelve o'clock, for some reason, I woke up and heard someone mumbling. I knew that it must be getting on toward the time to move out. In a minute or two, Sergeant. Ward, came over and whispered for us to get up. It was already getting cold that night and all the clothes that I had on felt good. I had no more than felt around the hole and put on all my equipment, before the order came to assemble and we filed off through the trees.

When we got to the road, G Company was already moving out. They were to take another road into the town that we were to attack. We waited for about half an hour and then began to walk in the same direction that G Company had taken. It was easy to tell the direction of the front by the burning towns and haystacks. There were fires all along the horizon lighting everything up as if it were day. Rockets were going up into the night sky and then you could see tracers go into the sky toward the strafing planes. Occasionally, you would see the planes come out of the sky towards the ground.

It wasn't long before we came to the first of the burning towns. We waited in it for the time to pass so that G Company would have plenty of time to get around to another road. When we finally did start out, you could see the shadow of a plane pass the moon occasionally. Once, a plane came down to strafe something near us and we all dived for the gutters along the edge of the street.

Eventually, we moved out towards another of the towns that was burning,[32] but before we got to it, we turned off the road into an open field. We moved through the field parallel to the town and as we did, we began passing men dug-in in the bushes to our left. They were men of the 39th Infantry Regiment that we were relieving for the time being. They had been spearheading the attack for the past two days and now it was our turn.

We stopped in the middle of the field, about two hundred yards from the edge of town, and began organizing for the push off. I had just hit the ground to relax, when a machine gun opened up on us from the edge of the town. The machine gun fired for about two minutes and then the firing ceased. Someone yelled "is that GI's" and then a flow of curse words went back at him telling him to the effect that it was GI's. One of the heavy machine guns of the 39th had mistaken us for Germans. Only one casualty resulted from all of this firing and that was a fellow hit in the heel. In such a situation as we were in, the wounded man probably considered it a blessing.

E Company began moving out across the open field that was flat as far as you could see in the moonlight. Not even the slightest rise was visible from our position. My platoon was third from the front and

---

[32]Vettweiss.

after we had moved about five hundred yards across the field, a German burp gun[33] opened up on us. It didn't take us long to hit the ground. Although I fell on top of the bazooka shells, I managed to wiggle them out from under me so that my back wouldn't be sticking up so high. The field that we were laying in was a turnip field and many of the turnips were laying around us in piles. I tried my best to hide behind some of the turnips and I could hear the bullets hitting around me.

The burp gun stopped now and you could hear German rifles pop in the distance. A bullet went past just to the left of me. I felt pretty safe as long as the bullets were passing in front of me, but when they started going in front of me, and then in back of me, and also began hitting the ground and piles of turnips close by, I could only wish that I could crawl under my steel helmet.

No one had fired back at the Germans as yet, but pretty soon a bunch of shots began going out from the squads on the side and in the front. Then out from some place right in front of us, two Germans jumped up jabbering something and put their hands over their heads in a sign of surrender. One of our officers led them off and began questioning them. We finally cleaned them all out and started out again. Then, from the front of us, more shots started whining over our heads. We hit the ground again and must have lain there for what seemed like an hour before the Germans finally were cleaned out by another part of the company. When we began to move again, mortar shells landed amongst us. Some of the guys were hit by the mortar shells, but none were seriously wounded

---

[33]Most German machine guns were referred to as burp guns because they fired at a rate which was about twice as fast as American machine guns and made more of a burp or zip sound than the rat-a-tat-tat sound of American guns.

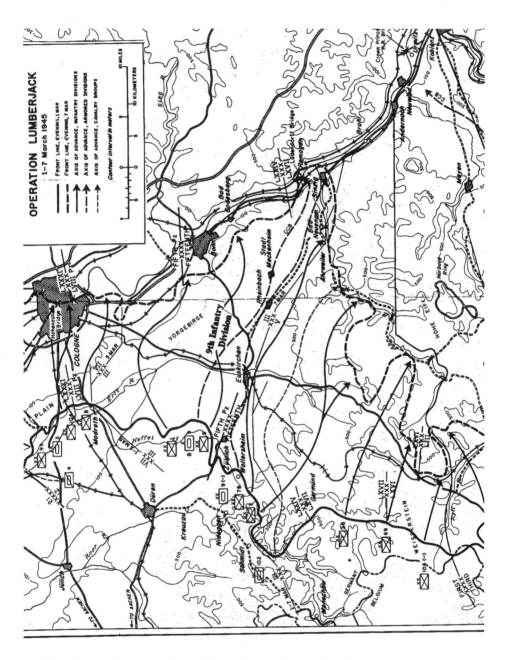

Map 3 - Advance of the First Army From The Roer to the Rhine
(Rotate map for better viewing)

44

Chapter 4

Attack on Geich
(March 2)

We moved past the place in the field where the mortar shells were landing and, after that, the shells landed in back of us. After crossing two wide German defensive trenches, we finally entered the town. As we did, we met G Company coming in on the other street. We cleared the town house by house and when we came to one end of it we noticed Germans trying to crawl across the field to a patch of woods. We fired at them and they would lay still for awhile and then start crawling again. Finally, our platoon sergeant brought up a machine gun to spray the field and my squad went on to another part of town to clear out more houses. There were no civilians in the town and only a few German paratroopers to defend it. They were so scattered that they did not put up much resistance. It was well after daylight now. We had finished clearing the houses and were standing in the street talking when mortar shells began hitting in the street. We went around the house to the back yard where there was a little more cover. Then Sergeant Ward sent four of us to an old mill to serve as an outpost in that end of town. From where we were located, we could see across an open field to another town[34] located about a mile away.

We were out to the side of the mill behind a wall and by the side of the mill stream. Mortar shells kept falling around us and then artillery shells came screaming in, but they were landing behind us. By this time, it was about eight in the morning, so we began to take time out for breakfast. Two of us stayed on watch while the other two ate their rations. It was Hart's birthday. He was nineteen today, and when I had finished my breakfast, I came outside to tell him about a safe place that I had found between the two buildings from which we

---

[34]The ancient German city of Zulpich.

could watch the field. Just at this time, a mortar shell landed so close to us that it spun us all around and knocked us off our feet. A piece of shrapnel (shell fragment) caught me in the back before I hit the ground. It didn't hurt, but only felt a little numb, as if someone had stuck an ice pick or a sharp stick in my back. Hart asked if anyone was hit and I told him a piece had hit me in the back. Boshell jumped up and looked at my back. He saw the hole in my jacket so he went with me over to the building where Sergeant Ward was located. Ward then took me down the street to try to find a medic, but no one knew where any were at this particular time. Finally, we found a medic from G Company and he put a bandage on my back. He said that the wound was made by a piece of metal about the size of the end of my finger. It was not bleeding because the fragment went straight in and the skin came back together. When the mortar fragment hit me, I was wearing a field jacket, a wool sweater, a wool shirt, a wool undershirt and a cotton undershirt. All of these layers of clothing probably helped slow the fragment down somewhat.

The medics put a medical identification tag on me that said that I was wounded at Geich. This was the first time that I knew the name of the town that we were attacking. During the time that I waited at the aid station, there were two wounded Germans laying on the porch. One of them was unconscious and very pale. The medics had treated the men and they were also waiting to be evacuated to a hospital. I was told to go over to the company command post (CP) to wait for an ambulance.

I found the CP in an old farm house in the middle of the town[35] and I waited there for some kind of transportation. Captain Petty was there along with Captain Craft of G company. They were taking it easy and waiting for either the Germans to counterattack, or for the companies to get orders to move out again. They explained that the

------

[35] Strange as it may seem to most Americans, German farmhouses are located in towns.

road into the town had not been cleared, so there was no way that an ambulance could come in to pick up the wounded. German shells started whistling in again and I saw the first one hit the roof of the barn across the courtyard of the farmhouse. This shell didn't even break the window in the house where we were. The second shell hit across the street and this time it sent a shower of glass down on Captain Craft. No one was injured by the shell or the glass, but I was getting pretty uneasy. All the time that I was waiting I was thinking that, even though my wound did not seem to be serious, I was going to be killed here at the CP while I waited for an ambulance to evacuate me. The shelling didn't seem to worry the two captains so I gained a little confidence from them.

In about two hours, another sergeant came into the CP and said that there was a weasel[36] across the street that they were going to use to evacuate the wounded men. So I went across the street and got on the weasel. The driver was hurrying to get out of town before the next barrage of shells came in and I was all for that. There were two litter cases on the weasel that had been hit by one of the shells. One man had been hit in the arm and one in the leg. They were pretty ugly flesh wounds, but neither wound appeared to be life threatening.

We got out of town before any more shells came in and went back across the wide open field that we had crossed before daylight that morning. The battalion aid station was in the last town that we had left the night before. My wound was checked but my dressing didn't need changing since my wound wasn't bleeding very much. At the battalion aid station, we were put into a regular military ambulance and sent back to another aid station in Nideggen. The ambulance was warm and I realized that it had a heater in it. This was real luxury for the battlefield.

There were two wounded men on this ambulance from the heavy weapons unit to which Bertrand had been assigned. I heard them

---

[36]Small tracked cargo vehicle.

talking about the fighting the night before and how a new guy in their unit had been killed. I knew then that Bertrand was dead. Although the men that were talking did not know the name of the man that had been killed, I just had a feeling that it was Bertrand.

At the next stop, while we waited for another ambulance, we were given some sulfa tablets to swallow. We were then moved out to another division aid station which was set up in a tent. At this aid station I was given a tetanus shot and put on an ambulance going to a field hospital. The ambulance traveled through the mountains and across the Roer for about two hours. Stolberg was one of the first towns that we passed through and we went on from there to a field hospital located in the outskirts of Aachen.

We stayed at the field hospital only long enough to get our records straight and for the medics to fill out a lot of forms. At this hospital, we received our first Penicillin shot. It was the first Penicillin that any of us had ever received since Penicillin had only been developed the year before and was being used almost exclusively for combat wounds[37]. We had all received a lot of shots in the army but we had never seen a needle or syringe this big. The entire shot was injected into our arm. We heard over the radio, while we were there at the hospital, that the Ninth army had reached the Rhine River.

It wasn't long before we were put into another ambulance and carried across Aachen to an Evacuation Hospital. The Evacuation Hospital is a place where they treat and keep the wounded until they can get a train to take them back to a General hospital. We were taken to a waiting room which was actually a large hallway at this hospital. The floor was filled with stretchers containing wounded and dying men. In the midst of all these wounded men, there was a German woman sitting on a bench along the wall holding a little child about one year

---

[37]Penicillin was developed by the English and Americans on a crash basis so that it would be ready for the Invasion of France. The allies felt that an anti-biotic such as Penicillin could save the lives of many men who would be wounded during the invasion.

old. He had been hit by a piece of shrapnel right above the eye or possibly in the eye. He was crying and the mother was sobbing. I overheard a major as he came over and spoke to a captain that was administering to the GIs. The major told the captain that they had to get the woman and child out of the waiting room before it affected the men that were laying all over the place on stretchers.

Wounded German prisoners were mixed in with the Americans in the waiting room. Some of the GIs offered the Germans cigarettes and chocolates, but then some of the other GIs took exception to this and a row broke out for a second or two. It was over as soon as it started and was something that I grew accustomed to among fighting men. Our nerves were stretched to the breaking point. The slightest disagreement could become a violent argument and then be over in the twinkling of an eye with no hard feelings.

It was almost eleven o'clock that night before we finally got a bed, but first they had to look at our wounds and give us another shot. There was always Sulfa pills that went with every shot of Penicillin that they gave us. The beds were luxuriously clean with two white sheets and a clean white blanket over the top. We were all so dirty that some of the boys wouldn't crawl between the sheets, but lay instead on top. I couldn't resist the sheets myself and I crawled under them and finally got warm for the first time in three days. It had been awfully cold that day and it had snowed on us all during the day. However, here in Aachen, out of the mountains, no snow had fallen.

The next morning I washed up really good for the first time in many a day. I hadn't brought any thing with me, so I couldn't shave. I went to breakfast and who should I meet there but Jenkins, one of the fellows from my squad. He had been evacuated for bad feet. Later on in the morning, I also met Gearhart who was also from my squad. Gearhart had been wounded by the mortars as we crossed the turnip field to attack the town of Geich. He had been hit in the arm by a shell fragment, but his wound was not serious.

One of the first things that most of us tried to do this morning was to write a letter home to our families to let them know that we were OK. One of the men said that his wife had a bad heart and he was afraid of what would happen to her when she got the telegram from the War Department. This was something that we all dreaded and we hoped that somehow our letters might get through to our loved ones before the telegram was delivered[38].

At about ten o'clock, after we all had another penicillin shot, we left to catch the ambulance train.

------

[38] I found out later that my mother was terrified when the Western Union boy brought the telegram. She wouldn't open it until she called dad and he rushed home from work with the publisher of the newspaper on which he worked. This was what we all dreaded, the effect on our family if something happened to us. They must have felt so helpless sitting at home waiting for some word from the front. I am sure if they had known what was really happening at the front, and what our chances were, they would have been even more terrified.

Chapter 5

The Hospital in Liege
(March 3-16)

We went to the train in a convoy of ambulances, or you might say, just a steady stream of ambulances. At the train, those of us who could walk were put into a sitting coach, since we did not have to be carried on to the train in stretchers. The stretchers cases were placed in specially outfitted cars. The chairs were very comfortable and there was a table between each row of chairs. I was really impressed by all the attention that we were getting from the aid men and nurses that were on board the train. They gave us more shots and dinner and, after a long wait, we finally pulled out of the Aachen train station.

We took the long route to Belgium by going up through Holland, which seemed to be a nice quiet little country. All the houses were modern and clean and there was little or no war damage in this part of the country that we could see. We passed through Maastricht, Holland late in the afternoon and before long we were rolling into Liege, Belgium. Liege is quite a large industrial town with many coal mines nearby. It was after dark before we got off the train and onto the ambulances that were to take us to the hospital. The ambulances carried us through the blacked-out streets of Liege, but with their own lights burning. We crossed the Meusse River and, about two blocks passed the bridge, we turned into the 56th General Hospital. It was quite a rambling structure with many different buildings that didn't appear to be hospital buildings at all. It was, in fact, an old factory of some kind that had been changed so drastically that you could not recognize what it had been before.

After a doctor looked at our charts, he assigned us to different wards. All those that required surgery went into a certain ward. I was sent to the surgery ward and finally got to bed for a little sleep.

The ward was plenty crowded with beds all down the middle and every place else. I spent the next day sleeping and being examined. They took a lot of X-rays and kept asking me if I could breath OK. They evidently thought that the shrapnel might have gone into my lungs. But I was having no problem breathing so I spent the day waiting for them to remove the shrapnel from my back. Finally, at about eleven o'clock that night, they gave me a shot of morphine and took me, along with five others, to the operating room.

We were seated in a waiting room along with several German prisoners. We were all wearing surgical gowns so it was difficult to tell the difference between the Germans and the Americans. People were taken to the operating room pretty steadily for awhile and then there was a long period that they didn't take any of us. We got to wondering if maybe they thought we were Germans, so I went up to the desk and told the duty nurse that we were Americans. Sure enough, she thought that we were Germans, so she apologized and pretty soon they came and took us to the operating room. The operating room was just a huge old warehouse room with many surgical tables lined up throughout the room. Doctors were working at each table. They took me to one of the tables and the doctor looked at my X-rays and examined my wound. Then he very quickly took the shrapnel out of my back. The wound was evidently not very deep and I noticed very little pain, but I was so much under the influence of the morphine that I really did not know what was going on by that time. The doctor asked me if I had any other wounds and I told him no, so he sent me back to the ward. I slept all the next day and for two or three days after that because of the morphine and exhaustion. During that time, I was moved from the temporary surgical ward to a permanent recovery ward.

As soon as the morphine wore off, I had a little back pain, but for the most part I was up and around again. I went to the shows which were held in the Red Cross room and used the Red Cross stationery to write home. Sometimes the German buzz bombs[39] would go right over the hospital, since Liege was in the corridor referred to as *Buzz Bomb Alley*. These were the original V1 rockets and the putt-putt sound they made as they went overhead reminded me of a motorboat [40]. The hospital staff was terrified of the flying bombs, since a few had actually fallen in Liege. Most of the wounded men in the ward just laughed at the staff since they figured that their chances of being hit by a buzz bomb were pretty small compared to the dangers that they had just left at the front line. None of the bombs hit Liege during the period that I was in the hospital.

There was a nurses station in our ward and there was usually always a nurse on duty. However, sometimes late at night, they seemed to disappear. During the first few days, there were several critically wounded men and amputees in our ward. One boy in the bed next to me had lost his leg just below the knee from a rifle shot. Several times he woke me up at night screaming in pain and I would get up and adjust his leg to ease the pain. I had heard of the awful odor of gangrene but I had never smelled it myself until I worked with his unbandaged leg. The odor was nauseating and added to the discomfort and shock that I felt. We tried to cheer the guy up and he was taking his loss of leg pretty well since it meant the end of the war and a trip home for him. He said that the leg had been amputated in a field hospital where they usually didn't do such surgery. The doctor had told him that he had only been able to save a leg with a wound such as his once before and that was with a German soldier. Another man across the ward screamed in pain all of the time. I was told that he had been emasculated by a shell fragment. The men such as this with very serious wounds were evacuated to Comm. Z[41] very soon after they arrived.

---

[39] The German V1 rockets were being fired at England and Antwerp. Antwerp was the Allies only supply port other than Cherbourg.
[40] The German V1 rocket made the putt-putt sound but the V2 rockets were more like conventional rockets and made no sound as they passed overhead.
[41] Comm Z, which is short for Communication Zone, here at Liege usually meant England. although occasionally people were evacuated to Paris.

We were able to get *The Stars and Stripes* newspaper each day at the hospital. On March 8th there was much excitement because the newspaper reported that the First Army had seized a bridge across the Rhine on March 7th. The news report did not say where the bridge was located but the newspaper speculated that it was at Remagen, since all news from that part of the front had been blacked out. The same newspaper said that the 9th Infantry Division was fighting to clear the town of Bad Godesberg on the Rhine just above Bonn (See Appendix for this copy of the Stars and Stripes).

I got a pass from the hospital one afternoon and went down across the bridge and into town for a little while. I shopped in some of the stores but the prices were too high for me to buy anything. I was short of money anyway, since I had not been paid since I left the states[42]. I stopped at the big Red Cross Club near the bridge and had coffee and doughnuts. I was surprised that you had to pay for doughnuts in the club, since I had never before paid for anything that I received from the Red Cross. I was told that it was the Red Cross policy to charge for doughnuts in the rear area since there were many foreign troops that used the clubs along with the Americans. There were a large number of Polish soldiers in the club at the time that I was there.

After I had been in the hospital ten days, I was declared OK. I left the hospital along with the same men that I had come into the hospital with ten days before. These were also the same ones who had been in my ward. We traveled by truck to Verviers where the 3rd Replacement Depot was located. I thought that it was an amazing coincidence that the men that were in the same ambulance going to the hospital should be on the same truck leaving it.[43] One

---

[42]We were not paid until the end of the war, but we really didn't need any money at the front.

[43] Actually it was no coincidence, it was army policy. Each hospital had a certain holding time for patients depending on how crowded they were. Those that could return to action, regardless of whether their wound was healed, were

of the fellows that had been in the ambulance going to the hospital was a tanker whose tank had been hit by an armor piercing shell. He had little spots all over him where the hot metal from the shell had hit him. They didn't attempt to bandage all of the places. Here he was on the truck with me going back to his unit. His experience made me realize that maybe there were some worse jobs in the army than being an infantryman.

It took us about an hour to get to Verviers. I hadn't expected to see Verviers again, but here I was once again, heading up to the Western Front. We went to an old factory building where the depot was set up. It was a depot for casuals (men returning to their outfits) and there were no new men there. All of the men at the depot had been wounded and were returning to their units. I guess because of this, they were very easy on us. We had the freedom of the town and there was never a roll call. There were good shows every night and a Belgian ice cream parlor across the street from the building. We had strict orders not to eat the ice cream because the milk came from cows that had not been tested for Tuberculosis. As you would imagine, no one paid any attention to the order. The trolley ran right in front of our door and any American soldier could ride it anywhere it went, free of charge. Verviers was practically undamaged by the war, although some bombs had fallen in spots around the town. The Belgian stores seemed to have more to sell than we remembered in the stores back home. There were camera shops, fur stores, dry good, and department stores, with practically anything you could want, for a price, and what a price. It was nice to look, but I had no money to make any purchases of the expensive goods. I did find a nice fountain pen and bought it at a nominal price. I told some of the

---

sent back to the front. At this time, the hospitals in Belgium had been reduced to a ten day holding period because of the number of casualties that they were receiving. At the hospital in Aachen we had all been classified according to the seriousness of our wounds. Those in my group were sent to hospitals in Belgium. The more seriously wounded were sent to hospitals in Paris where they would be kept for a much longer period of time. The extreme cases that probably would not return to combat were sent to England.

fellows about the French and German money that I had and they assured me that it was valid money. They insisted that I go to the military finance station located in the town and sure enough they gave me Belgian money for both the German and the French. It seemed so strange that the money of our enemy could still be valuable.

By now, we all knew that the First Army had crossed the Rhine at Remagen and we were all dreading going back to our outfits. We knew our units were probably taking a lot of punishment fighting in the bridgehead, but we did not know just how bad they were taking it until we got back. Going back to the front after being wounded is much worse than going up to the front for the first time. The first time you go up, you don't really know what to expect and there is a certain amount of adventure involved, but when you go back to the front after once being there, you know all too well what you will be facing.

After we were in Verviers about four days, we got our orders to ship out. We were loaded on trucks again and sent up to a forward replacement depot at Euskirchen. Euskirchen was a fairly large town, just beyond the place where I had been wounded. As we passed through Aachen we could see long lines of brand new tanks and all kinds of new armor. They were readying the equipment to be sent to the front.

Euskirchen, like all the towns between the Roer and the Rhine, had been just about leveled by our artillery. One of the buildings left standing was a school house where the forward depot was located. The depot had just moved there the day before and had not really gotten properly set up. There was a new shipment of men there that had just come in from the states and they were running around picking up any piece of junk that they could find for souvenirs. I wonder what they did with the souvenirs once they got to the front? I remember seeing a beautiful pair of German officer calvary boots, but what would an infantryman do with something like this?

While in Euskirchen, I ran into Sergeant Lynn Brown from E Company. I had not known Brown while I was in the company, but it was good to meet someone from E Company and we became good friends on the trip back to the unit.

We only stayed in Euskirchen over night. The next afternoon trucks arrived from the 9th Division, which we now knew was across the Rhine at Remagen. We left at four in the afternoon. It was only about twenty miles to the river from where we were, but soon after leaving town the truck convoy ran into extremely heavy traffic heading for the bridgehead. We had to slow down to just about a walk. The 1st, 78th, and 99th Infantry Divisions were moving into the bridgehead and had been moving in for almost two days. All along the roads there were signs saying "To the Bridge". It took us until almost ten o'clock to reach the 9th Division rear echelon which was still about seven or eight miles from the bridge. The rear echelon was located in a large soda pop factory and we spread our rolls in part of the building and got some sleep.

The next morning the traffic heading toward the bridge was much lighter and we made better time. All along the road before we got to the bridge we could see our anti aircraft guns. They seemed to be located about every fifty feet along the roads and in every direction. This was the greatest concentration of anti-aircraft that any of us had ever seen. They were located all along the roads near Remagen and overlooking the Ludendorff Bridge[44]. The convoys were moving up

---

[44]Many historians say that the concentration of anti-aircraft around the bridge at Remagen was the greatest ever used in the European Theater. At the height of the attacks on the bridge, sixteen 90-mm gun batteries were emplaced on the west bank and twenty-five batteries of automatic antiaircraft weapons were divided between both banks. It was very effective. The Germans sent plane after plane at the bridge without ever damaging it. Hitler even had V-2 Rockets fired at the bridge from their bases in Holland. From March 12 through March 17, eleven of the V-2 rockets were fired at the bridge. But, the rockets that had terrorized England went wide of their mark and did no damage to the bridge in this, their only use in a tactical situation. One rocket did hit a house about 300

to the bridge bumper to bumper, but the Germans never dared to attack them, although they were still sending planes against the bridge.

At the town of Remagen, you could hear our shells going into the German lines and the German shells coming back at us. None landed close to us and after a short wait, we crossed the pontoon bridge across the Rhine. The pontoon bridge had been thrown across the river upstream of the Ludendorff Bridge. The Ludendorff Bridge was being repaired this morning[45] and they were not allowing convoys to cross it. You could see it looming up through the fog and the smoke screen as we crossed. At this time, there were no barrage balloons above the bridge, but later on twenty balloons were put up to protect the bridges.

The Rhine is about 400 yards wide at Remagen and I was surprised at how narrow it was. I was expecting something much wider on the order of the Mississippi River in Louisiana. I couldn't help but compare the Rhine to the Arkansas River near Camp Gruber, Oklahoma, where I had so recently trained. After we crossed the Rhine, we followed it north through the town of Linz and to the foot of the Ludendorff bridge. After we passed the huge hill[46] at the base of the bridge, we turned away from the river and went into the high hills which surrounded the river. If there had been any place less ideal to cross the river, I don't know where it would have been since the bridge was a railway bridge and there were no roads leading from it.

---

yards from the bridge, killing 3 Americans. The Air Force also put up a fighter screen over the bridge to chase away the German planes. It was estimated that the antiaircraft units   around the bridge shot down 109 of the 367 planes that attacked the bridge.

[45]The Ludendorff bridge had been closed since March 13 for repairs. The Germans had fired all types of heavy artillery at the bridge seeking to destroy it but none had hit the bridge itself.

[46]Erpeler Ley

Chapter 6

The Remagen Bridgehead
(March 16-17)

Armor was of little use in the bridgehead near the river because of the dense forests and the high hills which ran from the river as far as you could see. The hills had to be fought for and taken by just the plain old rifleman. But he had plenty of help from the artillery. There was more artillery for the space in the bridgehead than any other place we had ever seen before.

At the time of my arrival, the bridgehead was about four miles deep and eight miles long. That wasn't much room to move around in, but General Hodges had already put five divisions into this small space and more were following every day. Although the bridgehead had been captured on March 7th by a platoon of the 9th Armored Division, the 47th Infantry had been rushed to the bridgehead the first night after the bridge was captured and was the first complete infantry unit across the bridge. In fact, the 47th Infantry was the first complete infantry regiment to battle across the Rhine since the Napoleonic Wars.

The 2nd Battalion kitchens were located just a little way from the river in an old hotel. All four company kitchens were located in the same building. I only stayed there at the company rear headquarters long enough to get rid of the excess equipment that I had been issued[47]. While there, I had a chance to talk to the mail clerk[48] and

---

[47] I lost everything when I went to the hospital so all of my equipment and personal effects were new. I never recovered anything that had been in my duffel bag. I particularly hated loosing my chrome plated safety razor and case that Lavonne had given me for Christmas. I still had the metal backed bible that she had given me since I always carried it in my pocket over my heart.

find out who was left in the company. The mail clerk was probably the most knowledgeable man in the unit regarding the status of various people and he usually knew immediately when someone had been killed or wounded. As I visited with him I would call off a name and he would tell me if the man was still there or what had happened to him. I found out that Hart was still in the company and had not been hit during all of the fighting so far. Sgt. Ward and Sgt. Roberson and most everyone else that I knew were gone. The mail clerk pointed out a stack of boxes in the corner of his room and asked me if I wanted any of that stuff. He said that it was undeliverable mail for people no longer with the unit or that had been killed in action. With all of the casualties that the unit had been having these boxes were starting to accumulate.[49] All he could do was give it or throw it away because there was no way to forward it. I thanked him, but I was a little repelled at the idea of taking someone else's mail.

After the short wait, I went up to the front line on the chow and ammo jeep. Dessert that night was to be fresh cooked sugar covered doughnuts[50] and we were carrying them in the jeep with us. They smelled so good that they made me hungry, even with shells bursting all around us. If at all possible, our kitchen always served hot food at the front line, even during the fighting. Usually we only had two meals a day, which consisted of breakfast early in the morning and supper late in the evening, after most of the fighting had subsided. The food was placed in insulated containers and carried to the front along with the ammunition, Clean mess kit trays were

---

[48] This was John "the barber" Travelise who was a legendary personality in E Company. Company E survivors still use his mail lists today for determining information concerning former members of the unit.

[49] The postal service had a policy that forbid packages to be mailed to an APO number without a written request for a particular item from the addressee. This was to prevent friends and relatives from sending a lot of unwanted gifts to men that had no way of using them or of carrying them on their person.

[50] Clarence Combs, one of the E Company cooks, had been a baker before entering the army and was partly responsible for the delicious baked goods that found their way to the front by way of the chow jeeps.

brought up with the food. Since we had no way to clean our mess kits, they were all kept at the kitchen where they could be washed and sterilized after every meal and brought back clean for the next meal. We all carried a large spoon in our pocket which we used for our eating utensil. We also carried a few K rations[51] and D rations[52] to fill in between meals and use in emergencies when the chow could not be brought to us.

It was a rough ride up to the company positions. The roads were bad and we were going fast to keep out of the way of the shells that were coming in. We came up to the saw mill where a hard fight had been going on for two days now[53]. There were four of our Sherman tanks knocked out at this one cross-road. The Germans had finally been chased over the hill and E Company was dug-in for the night in the woods on this side. It was already getting close to dark when I reached the second platoon.

Instead of being greeted by all of the old guys that I had left, I saw only strangers. Finally I saw Hart. He was glad to see me and I sure was glad to see him. He told me that most all of the old guys from the platoon had been hit and that now there were only four of them left. In addition to Hart, Dawson, our bazooka man, Mays, and Gerrard had managed to come through unharmed.

---

[51]K Rations were complete meals placed in a box about the size of a cracker jack box. The meals were designated for breakfast, dinner and supper. The breakfast contained a small can of scrambled eggs and bacon along with a fruit bar, Nescafe, sugar, and crackers. The lunch contained a can of pork loaf with apple and the supper contained a can of cheese. Sometimes there were little chocolate bars or chewing gum in the rations and some of the rations had powdered citrus juice or powdered cocoa.

[52]D rations were highly concentrated 4 ounce chocolate bars that contained cocoa, oat flour, and skim milk powder.

[53]This was probably near Willscheid.

Hart brought me up to date on what had been going on since I left the company[54]. He said that most of the casualties had occurred after they crossed the Rhine. Sergeant Ward had been wounded first and then Roberson had taken over the squad. Roberson had been hit only a day or two before, somewhere near Bruckhausen. Hart didn't think that either of them had been hit real bad.

All of the new guys had just come in that afternoon and had not ever been in action. Worse than that, they had been pressed into service during the past two days as litter bearers, carrying the dead and wounded back from the front. They were a completely demoralized and terrified bunch of guys[55]. Hart told me that Myers had been killed by a sniper in Bruckhausen. Myers and Roberson had gone upstairs in a house and Roberson had posted Myers and another man as lookouts on each end of the building. Myers had gone to one of the windows and was standing in front of it when he was hit and fell back into the room. One of the younger fellows that had come overseas with us had been with him when he was killed and had taken the loss pretty hard.

---

[54] After I was wounded at Geich on March 2nd, the 2nd Battalion had captured Obr. Wichterich on March 3rd and Frauenberg on March 4th. On March 5th, The regiment with first and third battalions leading, had sized a bridgehead over the Erft River. The Second Battalion went through Metternich on March 6th to capture Hermerzheim. On March 7th, The Second Battalion was alerted to cross the Rhine at the Ludendorff Bridge and at 0400 hours on March 8th, with Lt. Col. Maness leading the way, they became the first complete infantry unit of the 9th Infantry Division to cross the bridge. (At that time, the 9th Armored Division had only a few tanks and a few platoons of armored infantry at the base of the bridge in the vicinity of the railway tunnel that enters the Erpeler Ley.) After crossing the bridge, the Second Battalion attacked through Orsberg with E Company leading, up the surrounding hills to the vicinity of Bruckhausen, where the German counter attacks began in earnest.

[55] In the years since the war, I have thought a lot about this mistake that the army made with these new replacements. During the time that I was an instructor at the Command and General Staff School, I used this experience to warn other officers against the misuse of new troops in their first exposure to combat.

Since Ward and Roberson were gone, we had a whole new group of sergeants. They had all gotten their rank back at training assignments and had no experience leading troops in combat. We now had a 2nd Lieutenant for a platoon leader. He was 2nd Lt. W. Y. Emery and he seemed like a nice guy. He had been in the air force or some service unit, and due to the severe shortage of infantry officers, the army gave him a few weeks infantry training and sent him to the 9th Division. He had never been in combat before, and had little or no idea of what he was supposed to do. However, he was a good leader and we learned to respect his courage.

I had been in the Third Squad of the 2nd Platoon when I was wounded, but now Hart and I were put into the First Squad with some of the new men. The other three experienced men were placed in the Second Squad with the rest of the new men and we operated with only two squads because of the lack of experienced people to fill the squad positions (squad leader and assistant, two scouts, etc.) .

I went over and started digging a hole to sleep in that night. One of the new men shared the hole with me The ground was soft so we got a good size hole dug before dark and managed to get it fixed up pretty well so that tree bursts wouldn't come down into it. However, I didn't sleep much that night. The shells were going in and out so much that it seemed like they would run into each other in the air. Our own artillery was hitting just a short distance in front of us. I had never been so scared before in my life. My teeth were chattering uncontrollably. This had never happened to me before. Everything had been leading up to this moment since I had left the hospital. I knew that I was going to have to go back into combat and, after having experienced it once, I knew what I was facing. That constant living with death every moment. Now, it was even worse than I had anticipated. I was in the center of the front line, in a tiny bridgehead, with most of my friends gone. In addition to all this, I was in the midst of a bunch of strangers who were even more terrified than I was. Sergeants Ward and Roberson, two people I respected as leaders, were gone. Hart was the only person that I had been really close to that was still left. The fact that we were the most forward located troops on the Western Front in Germany, with the best of the German army being thrown against us, didn't make me rest any better. Just a little before I finally went to sleep, I heard bullets ricocheting off the trees over head.

I slept till around midnight when we were awakened to start the attack on the town of Vettelschoss. When we first got up, it was pitch dark and you couldn't see a thing. But in a few minutes it got light. The artificial moonlight had been turned on. This was the first time that I had seen anything like this. The artificial moonlight consisted of spotlights located far to the rear which were shined against the clouds so as to reflect down upon us. This artificial light actually made more light than natural moonlight would have made. We started out through the woods and there was a constant whine of shells going over our heads and landing just over the hill. As could be expected, with new men and new leaders, we were very disorganized stumbling around in the woods. Finally, we did get somewhat organized and started to move forward. After wandering through the woods for quite a ways, we were getting closer to where our shells were landing. Once, when we were stopped for a second, a piece of shrapnel (shell fragment) came buzzing back from one of the shells and hit the tree next to me. A slow moving piece of shrapnel sounds like an airplane propeller when it is coming at you and it seems to go so slow that you think that it will never land.

We got lost in the woods and were about to enter the wrong town before we turned around and went back and got on the right track. E Company now moved towards Vettelschoss along the edge of the woods and everything seemed mighty quiet in the town. Without warning, a German half track started firing down the road that was off about three hundred yards to our left. G Company was moving up this road toward the outskirts of Vettelschoss. There was much shouting and screaming from the G Company men. Evidently some of them had been hit pretty badly. Some of us yelled for Dawson to come up and fire the bazooka at the German vehicle. Lt. Emery stopped us from firing since if we did we would give our own position away. he told us to keep on moving through the woods in the same direction that we were going.

As yet, the Germans had not discovered that we were in the woods, so we crawled further into them and waited. At this point, the Germans started firing screaming meamies at us. This was our name for the rockets fired from multi-barreled rocket launchers[56]. They honk like a car horn when they are fired and they look like a red ball of fire as they make a great arch going through the air. They also make a swishing noise as they travel and, to the GI facing them, they were the most terrifying weapon the Germans had. I started praying and reciting the 23rd Psalm[57] (Thank God my Baptist Sunday School Teacher had made me memorize it). There was nothing else that I could do but wait and see where the rockets landed. The waiting was almost unbearable. These rockets landed a short way in back of us, but the concussion from them was so great that it picked me right up off the ground and set me back down again. I was beginning to think that these were my last minutes on earth. I was laying in a ditch of water and I was trying to get deeper into it. I could feel the cold water seeping into my boots, but that didn't matter much now. My

---

[56]The *Nebelwerfer*, or "Screaming Meemie," was a multiple barrel 150-mm rocket launcher mounted on wheels and fired electrically. It was a formidable weapon if fired accurately.

[57]*The Lord is my shepherd; I shall not want.*
He maketh me lie down in green pastures:
he leadeth me beside the still waters
He restoreth my soul:
he leadeth me in the paths of righteousness for his name's sake.
Yea though I walk through the valley of the shadow of death,
I will fear no evil: for thou art with me;
thy rod and thy staff they comfort me.
Thou preparest a table before me in the presence of mine enemies:
thou anointest my head with oil; my cup runneth over.
Surely goodness and mercy shall follow me all the days of my life:
and I will dwell in the house of the lord forever. *The Holy Bible*, King James Version.

squad had gotten mixed up and now we didn't know where our squad leader was.

Some more of the rockets started coming toward us but these also hit behind us. We were probably too close to the German positions for them to take a chance on firing any closer to their own lines. It was starting to get light now and we were afraid that the Jerries would see us in the woods and open up on us. We were now just on the edge of town and had gotten separated from our platoon leader and squad leader. Some of the men started crossing the street and moving into the houses along the far side. Before long we all followed and into the cellars we went.

We didn't carry much equipment, just a blanket or sleeping bag, a small collapsible shovel (entrenching tool), and a few personal items, but we always dropped these small back packs and extra equipment in the first house we entered. We did this when we were going to clear a town so that we could move faster. We would come back and pick up the packs after the town was cleared, that is, if we could find them. Our artillery was now shelling the other end of town and the Germans were firing back into our end of town.

We cleared out some more houses along the same street and went down into the cellars of these houses to take up defensive positions. We had hardly gotten into the cellars, when German tanks in another part of town started firing down the street at our tanks, which were just now moving into the town. A fierce tank battle started right there. Tank shells travel awfully fast and they whipped up and down that street for two hours, leveling every building on it. One of the German armored half tacks had been hit up the street and was blowing up sending shells flying in the air, but none of the shells were exploding. It looked like every house in town was burning and the roof was now off the building that we were in. The first house that we had gone into got a direct hit and one side of the building was knocked down onto the packs that we had left there. Sergeant Michel was our new squad leader and, during the shelling, he got me aside and told me that he had no combat experience and that he would welcome any assistance that any of us more experienced people could give him. Of course, at that time, I wasn't all that experienced myself, but I felt like an old veteran compared to most of the men around me.

There was a German family including some small children in the cellar of the house where we were located. This was the first time that I had encountered civilians up close during the fighting. Always before, the civilians had been evacuated ahead of us. Now, I guess there was nowhere to run. I asked these people how long they had been in the cellar and they said that they had been there for 9 days. We felt sorry for them and tried to treat them nicely. They seemed to be getting along OK without our help.

Finally, the Germans tanks left town and we started moving down the main street. Some of the other platoons had already moved through other parts of the town and had just now rounded up about sixty German prisoners out of a schoolhouse in the middle of town. There were still Germans holed up in the big church which was also in the middle of town and there were others down across the railroad tracks. A German train had been sitting in the station with steam up in its engine when we entered town. We figured the Germans must have brought up reinforcements the night before. Our artillery was really going to work now on the church and since we were only two houses down from it, the shells were landing much too close for comfort. I was standing in the doorway of a little building behind one of the houses when a shell fragment from one of our own shells hit the fellow standing next to me in the hand. At first he tried to shrug off the wound as nothing of importance, but then his hand started swelling badly and the medics had to evacuate him.

We finally got the whole platoon into the large house and I was posted as a lookout on the second floor. The roof and one side of the building was knocked out and I stayed crouched in a corner to keep the snipers who had been shooting at us from locating me. Hart came up with his BAR to help me out. It was reassuring to have Hart around. He had joined the unit back in November and had been at the front ever since, without receiving a scratch. In just the brief time that I had known him, I had learned so much from him. I knew that I had to learn as much as I could from people like Hart, if I was going to survive for any period of time at the front. From our position in the house, Hart and I could see Germans coming up the hill to surrender. Lt. Emory then took a squad of men down to clear out the buildings along the railroad tracks.

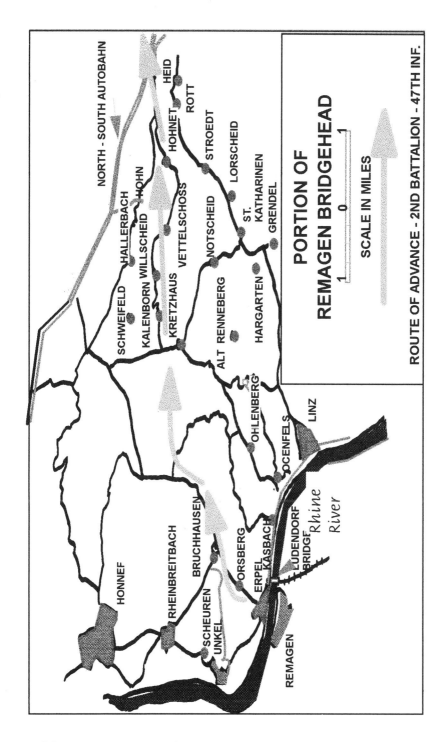

Map 4- Remagen Bridgehead - Showing Route of Advance of 2nd Battalion, 47th Infantry

Chapter 7

The Battle For Vettelschoss
(March 17-18)

The Germans in the buildings along the tracks surrendered right away without a fight. There must have been about twenty down there and they were the last Germans left in the town. At about that time, our artillery and planes spotted the German tanks moving off down the road away from town and started letting them have it, but they still managed to get away. Our artillery never seemed to do much damage to German tanks, but it was obvious that the Germans respected it All during the fighting there were about six Piper Cub observation planes in the air above us directing artillery fire upon anything that came into view. There were also forward artillery observers with the battalion that could radio back for artillery support. In addition, there were always plenty of P47 fighter/bombers within beckoning and they could really tear up the Germans. The P47s must have been very demoralizing to the Germans as they made their dive and loosed their bombs. The noise that they made was enough to startle even the nearby GIs. The Germans had now moved into the hills surrounding the town. Time and again we saw the P47's dive in and drop their bombs on their positions.

Vettelschoss[58] was cleared of Germans now, except for an occasional sniper, and we still had snipers a week later when we finally left

---

[58]On March 17, *The Marlin Democrat* carried the following dispatch from the Associated Press under the headline, Nazi Opposition Grows Near Rhine Remagen Bridgehead: **PARIS, Mar. 17 - The American First Army , battling to extend its Rhine river bridgehead at the center was meeting stiff resistance near Vettelschoss, seven miles east of Remagen, Allied headquarters announced today.**
My father set the type for this story without realizing that I was fighting in the town mentioned in the dispatch.

there. The people started coming out from their houses and the town came to life again. The people started milking the cows that somehow never seemed to be bothered by the shells or bullets. Although the town had been under artillery attack for ten days there appeared not to have been a single civilian killed in it. I think that shows how safe a good cellar can be, especially under artillery fire. Of course the cellars would not have been much protection against bombs and very large shells.

It was getting dark now and it seemed that most of the prisoners had been rounded up. At about this time a sensational rumor began to circulate through town that the bridge had fallen. We couldn't believe it at first but then there was verification at the CP from some of the ammo and kitchen people that had brought supplies up from the rear. We didn't know what effect that this would have on the battle, but we didn't think that it would have much, since the bridge had already been closed for a couple of days for repairs.[59]

Colonel Ward,[60] the new regimental commander, came by that night and said that we had done a real nice job in taking the town and that he was going to give us a rest[61]. It was about time that the unit

---

[59]We didn't know it of course , but General Hodges had not been satisfied with the direction of the fighting in the bridgehead, and on this day he relieved General Milliken, Commander of the III Corps, and replaced him with General Van Fleet. Two days before, General "Lightening" Joe Collin's VII Corps had crossed the river and assumed command of the northern part of the bridgehead.
[60]Colonel Peter O. Ward succeeded Colonel Smythe after Smythe was promoted and left the unit. Ward was a member of the class of 1931 at West Point and had come to the 9th Division from the 30th Infantry Division.
[61]The pause at Vettelschoss was due more to the fact that we had just about reached the departure point for the breakout attack, than to a desire to rest the unit. General Hodges was getting very restless at the restrictions placed on him by General Eisenhower. Hodges and General Bradley were not happy with the fact that General Eisenhower seemed to be placing all of the emphasis on the forthcoming crossing of the Rhine by General Montgomery in the north. Montgomery was still huffing and puffing and making elaborate preparations to cross the Rhine while both Hodge's First Army and Patton's Third Army were

rested, the 47th Infantry[62] had held the center of the bridgehead against fierce German attacks since their arrival on March 8. Most of the rifle companies were decimated and, like E Company, were now fighting with completely inexperienced replacements.

After we were sure that all of the Jerries had left town, we started looking for a place for the platoon to stay for the night. We went back to the school house where E company had set up their CP (Command Post) for the night. G Company and F Company were in control of the center and western part of the town, while E Company controlled the Eastern part of the town. My platoon was put into the very last house located towards the top of the hill overlooking the town and surrounding countryside. The hill did not appear to be natural, but was actually some kind of mining excavation or slag heap where the dirt had been dugout and piled up to make a high mound. From this mound you could see the surrounding territory for miles and you could also be seen for miles

Word also came around that the Catholic chaplain was going to have Mass that night up near the schoolhouse. Sgt. Michel, who described himself as a little guinea from Baltimore, asked me if I wanted to go to the service with him. I told Michel that I was Protestant myself and would wait for the Protestant chaplain. Michel replied, "Hell, I am too Blann, but I don't believe in being particular at a time like this."

Just before dark, I noticed that our artillery was firing shells that were exploding high in the air and dropping leaflets to the ground urging the Germans to surrender. The 2nd Battalion was now a finger sticking out into German held territory. The Germans held

---

across the Rhine and champing at the bits to go forward into the heart of Germany.

[62]The 47th Infantry, along with attached units, was awarded a Distinguished Unit (Presidential) Citation for its actions in the Remagen Bridgehead. A copy of this citation is printed in Appendix A.

ground on three sides of us, but other outfits were gradually moving around us and clearing them out.

After dark, we went out and dug holes for our outpost on top of the mound of slag. It was a wonderful observation point, but it could also be observed for miles around. We had to pull guard there that night, but other than a continuous shelling, nothing happened. During the night, I slept on a pile of potatoes in the cellar of a nearby house along with Hart and six other guys. The rest of the platoon slept upstairs. I was awakened several times during the night by shells landing close to the house. When this happened, the fellows up-stairs would come down and stay in the cellar with us until the barrage would lift.

Early the next morning, the boys that were on outpost came scampering in half scared to death. One shell had hit about a yard from their hole and created a hole about the size of the one that they were in. Another hit about five yards away from them and they had come into the cellar to escape any more shells that might fall. At several different times during the day, the guards had to come in to the cellar when it got too hot on the hill. When I went out to pull my shift, we tried to enlarge the hole and we did a fair job of it. The Germans fired airbursts[63] every once in a while, but none of them landed close to us.

Through our binoculars (I had picked up one-half of a binocular from some place) we could see a German tank burning on the next hill. We could also see other Infantrymen advancing across a field in front of us. Late that afternoon, we were upstairs in the house when a German 88mm gun[64] started shooting at us. An 88mm shell   is

---

[63] Airbursts are artillery shells that use proximity fuses so that they explode before they hit the ground. These shells send their fragments downward and negate the protection given by a foxhole.
[64] The 88mm gun was the best weapon the Germans had. It was usually mounted on their tanks, but it could also be mounted on a separate gun carriage and be used for antiaircraft artillery.

usually fired from a tank or some other type of armor and travels so fast that when you here the gun fire, there is just a zip and then it hits. We stumbled over each other into the cellar, but after a few more shells came in, some of the other fellows went back upstairs. Then I heard an 88 mm gun fire again and all of a sudden the house rocked and dirt fell on top of me from the ceiling and sides of the cellar. I heard the boys upstairs scrambling down again and I heard someone say that he was hit. It was one of the new fellows and he managed to get down the stairs and into the cellar. Hart also thought that he was hit, but it turned out that some flying plaster and stones had hit him. The fellow that had been hit now thought that he was dying and it was all that we could do to convince him that his wound in the upper chest toward the right shoulder did not appear to us to be life threatening.

It was dark in the cellar and some of the guys were using someone's flashlight to work on the wound. I passed my first aid kit and knife over for them to use. It seemed that a pretty large piece of shrapnel had hit him just above the heart. The wound was not bleeding much and no vital organs seemed to have been hit. The shell knocked out our phone and our radio was out, so one of the boys had to run over to the CP to get a litter team. Hart said that it looked to him like a ball of fire came in the window of the other room and it knocked them all a winding. We found out later that the shell actually hit a tree right outside the house.

Later that afternoon, the fellows on outpost had to leave the hole again, this time because of a sniper who was putting bullets into the hole with them. The Lieutenant and one of the men went out to look for the sniper, but another bunch of men had gotten him already. That afternoon, Lt. Emory took my squad over to another part of town to check some of the houses. The shell fragments were so thick on the ground in that area that it was difficult to walk. They were big jagged splinters of metal. Mixed all in with the fragments were leaflets printed in German encouraging the Germans to surrender. One of the new men in our squad stepped on one of the fragments and cut his foot. It didn't seem like much of a wound but this guy had been a nervous wreck ever since he had been in the unit. (He was the same fellow who had shared the fox-hole with me that first night back with the unit.) He was evacuated to the aid station and I never saw him again. We didn't stay in this area very long, and shortly thereafter we went back to the house near the mound of dirt.

One of the more disagreeable things about our stay on the hill was the dead bodies that surrounded us. Just outside the front door of the house where we were staying, there was the body of a dead German soldier. We usually ate our chow right beside him, so he didn't bother us too much. However, across the street in a shell hole there was a dead GI. This young fellow must have been killed the day we took the town and was probably from G Company since none of us knew him. He had been hit somewhere in the head because there was dried blood near his eyes. Unfortunately, he lay there for several days before a graves registration party came to pick him up. We were usually not allowed to move the dead because of the problem with later identification. This man must have been an assistant BAR man. Hart took the extra clips of BAR Ammo from him to replace his own. We didn't consider this scavenging since it was customary to recover weapons and ammunition from the dead as soon as possible. This custom led to some pretty terrible experiences at times when men had to go out and take the weapon off the bodies of their best friends. That night we moved across the street to the house beside which the GI was laying. It was a little unnerving to pull guard at night with a dead man laying beside you, especially one of your own men..

We usually took one hour tours of guard duty each night after we had been given the password and counter sign. The password would be something most Americans would know such as "New York" and the countersign would be "Yankees". Each man alerted the man that was to relieve him. That is, he would go awaken the man and see that he was wide awake before he left him. I had the only available watch in the squad. It was a little 21 jewel gold Bulova that my mother and dad had given me for high school graduation. We would pass this watch among us when we went on guard duty. The next morning I would get it back from the last guy to pull guard. If we were in fox holes, we just stayed in our own foxholes while we were on guard duty. Here in town we usually had to go outside the building or go to a spot near a shell hole that the squad leader had designated. If you had guard duty late in the night or early morning and didn't get awakened, you knew that some one had gone to sleep on his tour and failed to awaken you. This happened quite a bit here in Vettelschoss with all the new men in the platoon. I think some of them were just too terrified to get out of their holes and go awaken the next man.

My squad had moved into the house across the street to give us more room. It was a nice big house with thick walls. We always examined the walls to see if they were good and thick. This one also had a swell concrete and steel braced cellar. Most of the German cellars were full of canned food and we often tried it out as a supplement to our army rations. However, when we tried to cook something with the food we found it usually made us sick. Fresh eggs were a real treat when we could find them. But, more often than not, I would get sick from eating the fried eggs. I always figured the grease that we used was probably bad.

There were no civilians in the houses in this end of town. I don't know whether they had been moved out after we got there, or they had left before we came. There were a lot of clothes, trunks and various household items scattered in the yard. I never knew whether the people had started to leave with the stuff and had been forced to leave it, or what might have happened. I don't think any of the GIs had moved the stuff. Most of us had no way of carrying anything other than what we already had, so we weren't interested in picking up anything else. Mace found a guitar in one of the houses and would sometimes sit outside and play it when he had any spare time. But he didn't take it with him when we left.

Chapter 8

To The Autobahn
(March 18-25)

We had just gotten moved into the new house and situated in the cellar, when the order came to be ready to move out at a minutes notice. We waited for almost two hours and finally the order came for us to move to another part of town to take over positions vacated by F Company, who had moved out on to the side of a hill. All the towns in the distance were burning fiercely that night. Our artillery had fired a large amount of white phosphorous shells during the day and that had set just about everything on fire.

We found pretty good quarters to stay in. Of course the top floor of the house was knocked off like all the rest, but the cellar was in good condition. I also managed to find some sheets to sleep between. We spent another uneventful night and the next day D Company of the 1st Battalion moved their CP into the same house with us.

Hart and I found a motor bike in the shed behind the house and got it into working order. We rode it around a good bit during the quieter periods. We didn't often see correspondents or photographers but at this time there was a newsreel cameraman moving around town taking pictures of most everything in general. I don't imagine any of the pictures were ever shown in the states. We usually just rode the motorcycle up a trail to the top of a hill. It had very little power and would just barely climb the hill. One day I rode the motor bike right down through the middle of town. There was just one road through town and a dozer had cleared a path through the rubble just wide enough for the trucks to get through. It was usually jammed with traffic moving supplies up to the front. When I went roaring down the street on the motorbike, I ran trucks off the road and caused quite a commotion. Colonel Maness came running out of the 2nd Battalion CP yelling, "get that man's name." However, I was out of sight in a cloud of dust before anyone could catch me and no one at battalion headquarters ever found out who the driver was. As you might guess, Colonel Maness issued an order that night forbidding us to ride bicycles or motor bikes forever thereafter. So we never did it again[65], at least not when he was looking.

That afternoon I found some writing paper and an envelope and wrote to Lavonne. The weather had been pretty good and I was also feeling pretty good. Of course, I could give her no indication of where I was and what I was doing, so I just told her about Hart and I finding the motor bike and how much trouble we had keeping it running. I also told her about the camera that we had found and that Hart and I had been taking pictures. We were forbidden to send photographs home, but this was the least of our worries. At this time, we had no idea where we were going to get the film developed. Maybe we could have it done after the war.

That night, we were given instructions to move back to where we had been the first night, so we moved again. We now had an antiaircraft gun crew in the same building with us, but they didn't bother us much because we slept in the cellar and they slept up-stairs. Having anti-aircraft units around us was a novel experience in itself. We had never had them before this and we never had them after the bridgehead.

That night we were put on the alert for German paratroopers who were supposed to be dropped in the area. We pulled double guard as a precaution but nothing ever came of it.[66] The only incident that night, occurred when Donahue, one of the acting squad leaders, went

---

[65] One time about a month later I was riding a rickety old German bicycle around a farm yard when Col. Maness came up and asked me if I didn't know that there was an order that forbid bicycle riding. I told him that I thought that the order was meant to forbid riding on roads. He said, "no, it means anywhere, anytime".

[66] This alert for paratroopers seemed to come quite often, but I never heard of any ever being sighted.

out to the outpost on top of the mound to check two of the new fellows that he had left on guard. He crawled up to the hole and saw both of the guys curled up down in the bottom of the hole, neither of them maintaining a lookout. He exclaimed, "so..", and both of the men surrendered to him thinking he was a German. Needless to say, Donahue got pretty hot about this little encounter and went on for days about the quality of the people that they were sending to the front as infantrymen. He told everyone he met about having two of his own men surrender to him.

German planes dropped flares everywhere that night, but they didn't seem to find what they were looking for. It was sunny every day and our airforce was bombing right along in front of us, less than a mile away.[67] We stood outside and watched them during our off hours. They would come in and spot a target and make one low run over it and then they would circle back and dive toward it. You could easily hear their machine guns rattle and see them release their bombs. They carried three bombs and they would usually release them one right after the other. The planes were at it from sunup to sundown and strafed and bombed continuously.

Wednesday, March 21st, was a red letter day for me. I received my first mail that day since before leaving the states. I received six letters from Lavonne, four letters from mom and dad, and one letter from my aunt. They had been written during a period from January 26 to February 16 so they were pretty old. This didn't matter, they were mail and they represented a little bit of home. It's impossible to express the feeling that came over me when I realized that I finally had something from home. I didn't have any air mail stamps so I scribbled a V-mail letter to Lavonne to let her know the good news.

During our stay at Vettelschoss, we started a unit training schedule. Since almost the whole company was new to combat, we certainly needed to get organized to fight as a unit. The first day we spent

---

[67]These were planes of the IX Tactical Air Command.

doing a problem on taking a hill and using flanking maneuvers. That afternoon we went down to where some one had drug up a German Mark 6 tank.[68] The tank was used as a target in a demonstration on the use of the German Panzer Faust[69], one of the best weapons ever developed for knocking out a tank. The Panzer Faust was similar in principal to our own bazooka, except that it was about ten times more powerful and would knock a mighty big hole in any tank. We watched a demonstration of how our own bazooka shells bounced off the tank and then saw the size hole that the Panzer Faust made in the same tank. However, the Panzer Faust was not very accurate at a great distance, whereas the bazooka could be used from some distance away. The Panzer Faust was meant to be used primarily in city fighting or from a hiding place very near the target. From then until the end of the war, every squad carried a Panzer Faust and I did my share in lugging the thing around. There were three army photographers present and they made movies and took pictures of the demonstration. General Craig, the Division Commander, also came down and watched the demonstration. We kept up this demonstration and problem work every day to keep in shape, but no one really minded as long as we weren't shooting at Germans and they weren't shooting at us.

On Friday, I got more mail. This time I got letters from Lavonne dated March 9th & 11th. This meant that I had received a letter in

---

[68]This was the German Tiger II (King Tiger) Tank and was the largest German tank to see action during the war. It was the tank that the Germans used to spearhead the attack in the Ardennes during December of 1944. The Tiger tanks weighed 75 tons.

[69]The Panzer Faust differed from the American bazooka in that it was completely expendable. Once it was fired it was discarded. It consisted of two pieces of small diameter pipe that were fitted together for firing. The front piece of pipe had a large explosive charge connected to the end. Two small charges of propellant were loaded into the bazooka just before firing. The Panzer Faust did not have the range and accuracy of the longer barreled American bazooka that fired a rocket propelled shell. However, the Panzer Faust carried a much larger shaped explosive charge than the American bazooka and could penetrate 7 inches of armor. Both weapons were fired from the shoulder.

less than two weeks. I actually felt like I was part of the universe again. After receiving no mail for almost three months and then suddenly to be getting letters within twelve days was unbelievable. I had to write Lavonne and tell her about it. Now I had the luxury of answering her letters. She sent some stationery in one of her letters so I even had paper to write on. I borrowed an airmail stamp and sent the letter by air. For the first time, as an after-thought, I wrote "Somewhere East of the Rhine" just above the date. This way, if the censor passed the letter, she would know about where I was, since the only fighting east of the Rhine was at Remagen. Lt. Emory, our platoon leader, was responsible for censoring our letters at this time. I didn't know it at the time, but it was taking about five days for my letters to be postmarked at APO 9 after I wrote them. I suppose that this was due to the fact that they were slow in being collected and then they had to be censored and processed under front line conditions. Heaven knows when Lt. Emory found time to censor our mail.

We continued to take life easy in Vettelschoss until Saturday. On Saturday, I got a chance to go back to a quartermaster shower facility and get a good hot shower. When the unit was stationary, the company usually sent a few of us back every day for showers. The quartermaster unit would usually set up on the bank of a river and pump water from the river into large boilers connected to portable shower units. You discarded your old clothes, underwear and all, before you went into the shower. Then you picked up clean clothes as you came out of the shower. This time I managed to find some brand new trousers even though they were size 34 x 34. This was a couple of sizes bigger than I had ever worn before, but since we tucked the legs into our combat boots and pulled the waist up with our belts, it didn't really matter. I also got several more letters today in the mail

During this time, we heard that the Ninth Army and the British and Canadian Armies had crossed the Rhine, so we knew that we would not stand still much longer.[70]   The fighting had been slow in the bridgehead and, although we had been resting for one week, the companies that relieved us had only advanced about one mile up the road from where we were located.   Saturday night we knew well ahead of time that we were going to attack. We all wrote final letters home and, as soon as dark came, we started out down the road toward the front.   We went through a valley and wound around between the hills. Off to our right there was a terrific fire fight going on in the hills and the small arms fire was going over our heads from that direction. You could hear machine guns and rifles continually firing and our artillery was really going to town on targets in the hills. However, our artillery usually did that day in and day out so this was nothing unusual.

We passed through little burning villages and passed one stream where the engineers were laying a bridge. Our platoon took off from the road and crossed a pond of some kind by going over the levee at one end. We started up a hill and went through some bushes before we came to some buildings. We cleared out several farm houses but there were no Germans in them, so we kept going until we came to the top of a hill over looking the north-south Autobahn highway. The Autobahn had been the prize objective during most of the bridgehead campaign and it was now stretched out in front of us.   The place where we had met the Autobahn was about 10 km (6 miles) by air from the Rhine or about twice that by road. The location was 2 or 3 km north of the town of Neustadt and about 30 km by road from Bonn. This meant that the bridgehead was about six miles deep at this point.

It was now about midnight and we dug in and sent out sentries across the highway. Our artillery was keeping a red glow in the air just beyond the highway. I dug a deep hole in what was already a

---

[70]Many historians maintain that the First Army could have broken out of the bridgehead at any time but were restrained by SHAEF in order to let all of the armies get across the Rhine. The plan being to let all of the armies advance across Germany in one great offensive to end the war and meet the Russians.

shell hole and tried to get some rest. However, I managed to sleep only a couple of hours that night. We captured only two Germans during the night and they said that their units had left the day before. It was cold out in the open with no cover overhead. The only protection that we had was from our ponchos and these didn't insulate too well from the cold. There was a heavy frost during the night that made matters even worse. Sleeping under such conditions is difficult at anytime, but with shells going back and forth, it is almost an impossibility.

We spent Sunday, March 25, in the same holes awaiting our orders to move. The orders came to us just before dark and we picked up a supply of K rations. This meant that we would be moving out of reach of the kitchens for some period of time. There was also some canned celery soup with some sort of mechanism for automatically heating it in the can. This was something that I had never seen before so I had to try a can of it. The heating device made the soup so hot that I burned my mouth and didn't enjoy it all that much. Also, I had never especially like celery soup. We would be living on K rations and canned rations of this sort now that we were on the move.

The company moved out right away, but this time we went to an assembly area where we waited for trucks and tanks to move the whole battalion. We knew something must be up if they were going to move the whole battalion by truck. Some of the guys joked that they were pulling us out of the line and sending us to Paris for special guard duty. We had heard a mine[71] go off during the day and along the road we saw mines laying where the engineers had pulled them up. There was one GI laying there that had been killed when he stepped on one of the mines. We realized that this was the mine that we had heard earlier. These mines looked like plain little wooden boxes, but they packed plenty of power.

_____

[71]Mines make a different sound from other explosives when they are detonated. By this time we were able to immediately distinguish the explosion in the distance as having been made by a mine rather than artillery.

We waited till dark and then we got on the trucks; and, with the tanks leading the way, we went back towards the Rhine. Everyone joked about where we were going and some said that we were going back to Paris for a rest. However, we soon made a big circle and came back up to the front not far from where we had started, but this time we were across the super highway. We had traveled about two hours and several miles but we still were not more than a mile away from where we had been when we started our trip. I don't know the exact reason for this move, but the Autobahn does funny things to the small roads in the area. We were probably just maneuvering to get across the Autobahn by road and into position for an attack to break out of the bridgehead.

We now found ourselves in the 60th Infantry Regiment's area and we entered a little town that the 60th had already taken. We started to bed down for the night and my squad was placed in a schoolhouse with two old maid school teachers who were literally terrified out of their wits. Some of the German speaking guys tried to get them to calm down by assuring them that we weren't going to harm them. Although I never saw or heard of an atrocity being committed by GI's against the civilian population, I could understand their fear of these strange soldiers. Anyway, their concern about us didn't last very long since, before we had gotten settled for the night, Lt. Emory came around and told us to saddle up and to get ready to take another little town that was just down the road.

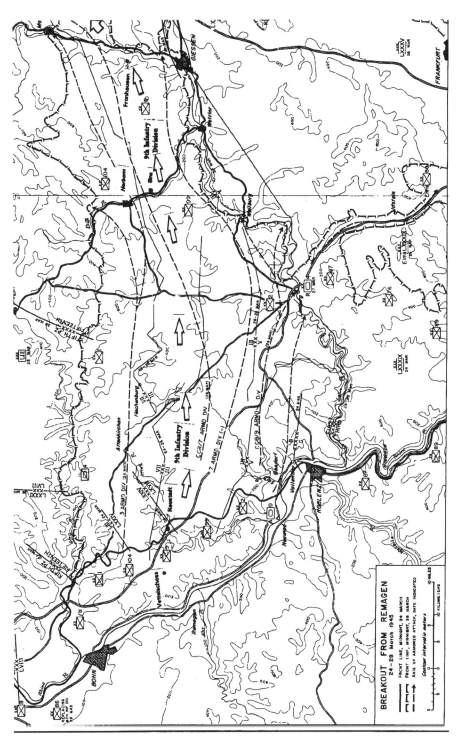

Map 5 - Breakout From Remagen Bridgehead

87

Chapter 9

The Breakout
(March 26 -28)

The little town that we were to attack was named Peterslahr and it was only about a half-hour march from the town that we were in. We went into the town straight down a road. My squad was to take one side of the street and another squad was to take the other side of the street[72]. We got into the first house without any trouble and kept on going from house to house. It was pitch dark and we had to use flashlights to look into each of the rooms of the houses. When we cleared a town, every house had to be searched and every corner of it examined. We kept on going through the town and, with the exception of our boys shooting the locks off of doors, there was no opposition. We passed several German army cars in the street that had rifles and other weapons still in them. They looked as if someone had just stepped out. I found a military map of the area in one of the vehicles that had markings on it in pencil. It looked as if someone had just laid it down for a moment and disappeared. There were also German army motorcycles laying around in the streets ready to go. By four o'clock in the morning, we had the town cleared. Only four German soldiers were found in the whole town. We all bedded down until morning and finally got some sleep.

The next morning we heard a wild rumor that the 3rd Armored Division (nicknamed *Hell on Wheels*) had gone around us on the left and that the 7th Armored Division had gone around us on the right and that the Germans were pulling out of the line in front of us.[73]

---

[72]Because of the shortage of experienced people, the platoons had been organized into two squads instead of usual three, when they were reconstituted in the bridgehead.

[73]The breakout had actually begun on March 25th but the armored divisions were not committed until late in the day of the 25th (Third Armored of the VII

We didn't discover that this rumor[74] was true until noon. By then we had marched through Burglahr and Overfahr and several other towns without being fired upon.

Before dark set in that night, we had gone seven miles and passed our days objective by a couple of miles. At one time that afternoon, we were forced to stop and wait almost two hours on top of a hill for our new objective to be given to us. Colonel Maness, the battalion commander, came up in his jeep and spoke to some of the officers and you could see that the officers were kidding each other and in a pretty jovial mood. Once while we waited, a small deer sprang up from the bushes and someone took a shot at it. I couldn't but help associate myself with the deer and wonder why men got pleasure out of stalking and killing other animals. I had been playing at this game for a couple of months now and didn't find any pleasure in it at all.

From the hill, we could see in front of us long dust streams fading into the horizon that were made by columns of tanks as they raced across the broad landscape. In the distance you could also see and hear planes strafing and moving further and further away from us. They looked like so many hornets attacking some prey on the ground. This was modern warfare in its finest hour - when the breakthrough has been accomplished and the armored units are moving forward at top speed. Most of us had joined the unit in Germany, so this was the first time that we had experienced such an event and we stood thrilled and amazed at the awesome might of an American army being unleashed at its full power.[75]

Corps on the North toward Altenkirchen) and early on the 26th (Seventh Armored southeast in the direction of Weilburg). On the 26th of March, the III Corps, commanded by Maj. Gen. James A. Van Fleet and, made up of the 7th Armored, the 9th and the 99th Infantry Divisions, captured 17,482 Germans. The 9th Armored Division of the First Army's V Corps drove eastward toward Limburg on the same day against almost no opposition.
[74]There was usually some basis in fact for every rumor that we heard at the front. Someone had either heard the information at headquarters or on the radio.
[75] The group that we were observing from the hill was General Van Fleets III Corps occupying the center of the attack from the bridgehead.. Although the

We were finally given orders to move into Dottesfeld, a little town at the foot of the hill, and we moved into it like a triumphal party. Everyone was shouting and kidding each other about the lack of combat as we moved across the field into the town. When we stopped, we got confirmation that the Seventh Armored Division had broken out of the bridgehead. They were now seven miles ahead of us with nothing in front of them but open country. We had to wait overnight for trucks to catch up with us and we spent a peaceful night of rest far from the sounds of battle. After so many days at the front, with the constant noise of battle always present, the silence was heavenly. We spent the night without being disturbed by even the sound of a rifle being fired.

Tuesday, March 27

The next morning we got up pretty late compared to our usual time of arising. We cleaned up and had a hot breakfast, the first and last hot meal we would have for a long time[76]. Everyone was in a pretty gay mood when we got on the trucks and the tanks at about ten o'clock. The trucks were mostly borrowed from artillery units since

---

attack had begun on March 25th, only the infantry divisions (9th and 99th) of the III Corps had participated in the attack on the first day. On the 26th, the 7th Armored Division was ordered into the attack and the breakout began in earnest. After some initial delays because of craters in the roads and a mix-up with V Corps on which units could use the autobahn, the 7th Armored Division completely penetrated the German lines and broke loose toward Weilburg on the Lahn River.

[76]When the unit is moving long distances the kitchens can't operate. The Ninth Division prided itself in the number of hot meals it served, but even they couldn't prepare hot meals when the kitchen was on the road. Armored units took this into account by supplying their people with ten-in-one rations which contained rations for ten people in one large box. These rations were meant to be prepared by smaller groups of people such as tank crews and gun crews. However the ten-in-one carton was too heavy for the infantry to transport without vehicles. So we were always given the K ration or C ration which we could carry in our packs.

an infantry company has only one supply truck and a kitchen truck with trailer that are organic to the unit. We heard from one of the officers that the 7th Armored was now twenty miles in front of us according to the latest reports.

We started out in a long convoy stretching further than the eye could see with the battalion tanks and tank destroyers leading the way in front of us. We went along during the day passing long lines of wrecked German vehicles and abandoned equipment. There were dead horses and dead German soldiers littering the sides of the road. Most of the German army was horse drawn in 1945 and it seemed to us that most of these horses were now laying beside the roads[77]. In many cases the bodies of the animals had not been pushed completely off the roads and the tanks would grind them up as they went by.

We stopped once beside one of these destroyed German columns. This gave us a chance to prowl around through some of the trucks. In one of the trucks we saw cases of American fruit cocktail. We speculated that it must have been captured during the Battle of the Bulge.

In every town there was a huge crowd to greet us waving white flags. This was our first experience as a "liberating" army. Up until now, any Germans that we had met had been very quiet and subdued. In addition to the German civilians, there was also another group that greeted us along the highways. These were the liberated French, Italian, Russian and Polish prisoners of war. We saw one group come running across a field towards us waving caps, turning somersaults, and performing all sorts of joyous acrobatics. They reminded us of a troop of clowns. When they got to the trucks they had to talk to everyone and shake their hands. But of course we didn't understand what they were saying. Some of the guys would throw them cigarettes and chocolate and we would be on our way. The German

---

[77]These destroyed columns of German vehicles were evidently knocked out as they fled, either by the air force or our tanks.

women would be standing in front of their houses laughing and holding their babies to wave at us and acting more like we were liberating them than conquering them. Many of them were passing gifts of fresh bread, sausages, jams, cakes and other delicacies to the GI's. In one town someone liberated a box of cigars and we all road along with cigars (most of them unlit) in our mouths looking like a bunch of Chicago gangsters.

We went on all day like this, only stopping when something in the road would cause us to stop. Occasionally we stopped to let the vehicles of another unit pass in front of us. There were different outfits going up all the roads and every once in a while we would run together and have to wait until the other passed. I don't think any one knew just where we were going that day. I had a big map of the area on which I was following our progress and we were just making great big circles, while all the time we were moving steadily eastward. We went through wooded areas and great open fields. All along the roads there was carnage of every description. There were overturned wagons and dead horses laying every place. This horse drawn equipment was no match for an armored division often moving as fast as 30 miles per hour.

That afternoon we got lost in a big forest but, after much wandering around, we finally managed to get out of it and back onto a highway again. Late in the afternoon we passed some of the rear units of the 7th Armored Division, so we knew we must be catching up with the front line. At the town of Sinn, a few miles south of Helborn on the Dill River, we passed armored artillery which was still firing at targets ahead of them. The Germans were also still throwing a few shells into the town when we first arrived. Sinn was a nice town and to our amazement, the electric lights were still burning when we arrived. (It was too good to last, the lights went out for good around ten o'clock that night.) Electric lights were something that we hadn't seen in months.

We stayed in a beautifully furnished house that night and everything was so nice. We turned on a radio in the house and listened to the news from the armed forces network. The people in the house made us coffee and gave us bread and jam and fried eggs to eat. There was only one middle-aged lady and her daughter in the house and there was a whole platoon of us. It always seemed strange that most of the women were not afraid of us even though there were never any men in the houses where we stayed. I expect, under the same conditions back in the states, the women would be scared to death to be staying alone in a house with twenty soldiers, let alone soldiers from another army. Of course, we were always well behaved. So, maybe they saw us for what we really were, just a bunch of frightened, homesick kids, most of whom would still have been at home, or in school, under normal conditions.[78]

Wednesday, March 28

The next morning we were awakened very early and sent out to guard bridges on the outskirts of Sinn. The Seventh Armored had already pulled out the night before and they were twenty miles ahead of us again. We had gone sixty four miles by road the day before and thirty miles due east towards Berlin. We knew that we were really rolling now. It was close to eleven o'clock in the morning before all of the 7th Armored Division had moved past us and we could take out after them. You could see their tanks spreading down the roads at their maximum speed of thirty miles an hour trying to keep up with the front elements of the division. It was hard to comprehend how fast an armored division could move in a breakout situation such as this. I stood and watched and marveled at the strength of such units. As I watched, a lump came into my throat just as it used to do when I was a child watching a parade and the flag came by.

---

[78] Some latter day historians (mostly British), quoting German sources, have accused the American Army of committing attrocities against the German civilians, I certainly never saw anything that remotely resembled an atrocity and I never heard any rumors of such occurring.

Today we rode tanks all day long. We stopped a good while before dark and found a place to sleep. It was the same story as the day before except that today we didn't even catch up with the armored units. We were told that they were still over twenty miles ahead of us. It was so dusty that day riding tanks that we were covered with dirt. We had to dust it out of our hair and clothes before we could even start to wash up. Our steel helmets served as wash basins and we would pour water to drink and to wash-up from the 5 gallon water cans that were brought up every night. The tankers wore goggles and they looked so strange when they took them off with their faces covered in dust except for where the goggles had been.

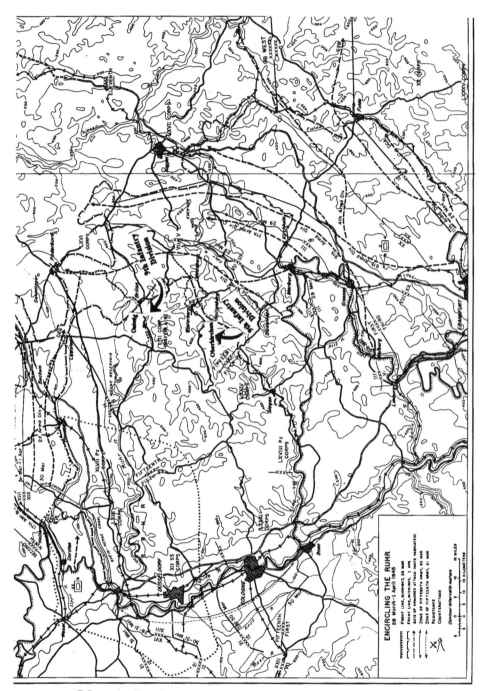

Map 6 - Encirclement of the Ruhr Industrial Area

Chapter 10

Toward The Ruhr
(March 28-April 2)

That night we stopped in the little farming town of Fronhausen in the vicinity of Marburg. The 2nd Platoon stayed in the headquarters of the Gestapo and the Nazi Party in the center of town. We had plenty of Nazi Party stationary to write letters home and also a typewriter with which to write them. We stayed in Fronhausen for two days waiting for the rear elements of the Ninth Division to catch up with us. We didn't mind this delay at all.

It was while we were in Fronhausen that the Third Armored Division, one of the three armored divisions of the First Army (VII Corps)[79], cut off the Ruhr pocket. Other parts of our armor went on seventy miles ahead of us. We weren't far from the area that had been cut off in the pocket, so that seemed to be the logical place for them to send us. We enjoyed the rest in Fronhausen, but on the afternoon of the third day (March 30) we got on trucks of the 99th Division and headed about thirty miles north and into the Ruhr pocket[80]. We were to guard roads which the Germans might try to use as escape routes.

On the way, we went through the old city of Marburg and as we passed we could see its old castles and buildings still standing. The

---

[79] The Third Armored Division was commanded by General Maurice Rose. In all of the confusion, General Rose was captured and killed by a German tank crew on March 30th near Paderborn. The linkup between elements of the 2d Armored Division of the Ninth Army and the 3d Armored Division of the First Army, which sealed off the German Armies in the Ruhr pocket actually took place at Lippstadt on Easter Sunday, April 1, 1945.
[80] Since the landings in Normandy, the Ruhr industrial area and not Berlin had been the objective of the Allied Armies in the west. The allies realized that the capture of the Ruhr area would effectively knock Germany out of the war.

town seemed to be in fairly good shape except for the areas along the railroads where everything was flattened. Marburg was supposed to be one of the oldest cities in Germany and it really looked beautiful that day. We moved up along the Lahn river and into the vicinity of Berleberg.

Just after we crossed the Lahn River, the road went up a long hill and we overtook some German civilians carrying all of their possessions in horse-drawn wagons. The horses appeared completely exhausted and unable to move any farther. It was just another of the very depressing sights that we were seeing every day. All of Germany was in complete turmoil by now and civilians of all nationalities were fleeing on the roads ahead of the armies.

We moved into the little village of Beddelhausen and out to the outskirts into a little rural school house. We went up to the attic of the school and made our beds for the night. Hardly had we gotten into them before they pulled us out and took us to a place about ten miles away. Here, they put us on the side of the road to knock out any German tanks that might try to break through and escape the trap. Everything was all confused and no one knew exactly where the Germans were and which way they might be coming from. I'm sure the Germans had no idea where we were. We heard that the 1st Division, following behind us that day, had come through a town that we had already passed through and were ambushed by three hundred Germans and three tanks. They had been forced to fight their way through the town. One of our own tank destroyers moved up one of the roads about two miles away from us that night and the Germans waylaid it and knocked it out. In the confusion, we didn't get our holes dug till almost morning and even then we didn't get much sleep.

Sunday, April 1

It was now Easter morning, April 1, but it was a dreary, damp and cold day. There were four of us on outpost in the foxholes that we had dug and we went in shifts of two over to a farm house where we warmed up and had a little to eat. We moved out at about ten that morning to another little town (Elsoff), where we occupied a big house on the outskirts of town and put our outpost way out on a hill. There was a smokehouse near the main house that was full of hams and sausages. We didn't bother any of the food since we had pretty strict orders against taking civilian food. The army knew that we didn't need the food and the civilians did. If we took the food, the army would just have to bring up more food to feed the civilians. Somewhere in this farmhouse I lost all of the pictures from home that I was carrying. I didn't discover the loss till after we had left and I was heartbroken over loosing these treasures from home. Now I had no pictures of my family or Lavonne.

Monday, April 2

We got a fair nights sleep that night, although we did have to go out on the outposts for an hour at midnight. Nothing much happened during the night and the next morning (April 2) we pulled out bright and early. We went on trucks for about five miles and then we got off the trucks and went across country on a little unpaved road through some woods and down a steep hill to a paved road. The tank and tank destroyer platoons followed along behind us all the way. E Company was in reserve this morning, which meant that F and G Companies were leading the way in the attack. We stopped at a crossroads and went up on the side of a hill where our platoon dug in to cover the road. The tanks and TDs pulled off the road and into positions from which to fire.

While we were digging our holes, we saw three civilians coming down the road with a white flag. After they talked with Captain Petty for a little while, one platoon of E Company was sent into the town of Girkhausen, about three miles down the road from us. We understood that the civilians were negotiating the surrender of the town.

After about an hour, the rest of us in E Company crawled onto the tanks and rode into the town that had surrendered to us without a fight. The rest of the battalion had gone down the other road at the crossroads and we didn't know where they were at this time. When we reached the town, we went out to the edge of it to place our outposts. We had just gotten there when we were all called back again. We remounted the tanks and this time went to help G Company, which was caught in a fire fight and pinned down by some German units.

We rode the tanks for only a little ways until we came to another road junction. There we had to crawl off the tanks and get up on the side of the road embankment to watch for the Jerries. They were firing all around us, but since the embankment was in front of us, we weren't worrying too much about the rifle fire at this time.

We stayed along the road embankment for about an hour and while we lay there a cold rain began to fall. When we moved out again, we went down a side road towards where the Germans had cut down trees to make a road block. We cut through the woods while our tanks bulldozed their way around the road block. Just as we got to the other edge of the woods, there, in a broad open field about a half mile in front of us, were about fifty Germans.

They were walking leisurely up the hill as if they had no idea that we were anywhere near. They knew it pretty quickly though, as we all opened fire on them at the same time. The Germans all hit the ground where they had been standing. Our weapons platoon set up their 60-mm mortars and began firing at them. The mortar shells seemed to be landing all around the Germans but in the wet muddy ground they were probably not having as much effect as we would have liked.

I fired an entire bandoleer (6 clips of eight shells) of ammunition at the target in front of me. I was firing so fast that some of the grease and oil on my rifle started to smoke. At one time during the firing, I was startled by a sharp crack nearby that sounded like a German rifle. I turned quickly and saw that it was just one of our officers firing a carbine, which I suddenly realized, made a sound very similar to a German rifle.

Some of the Germans in the field made a run for the woods, which were several hundred yards off to their right side, and managed to get into them in spite of all of our firing. Lt. Emory called for my squad (2nd Squad) to follow him across the field to pursue the Germans. While the rest of E Company lay down fire over our heads, we ran across about four hundred yards of the freshly plowed, muddy field, into the woods on the other side. This was just about the hardest that I had ever run in my life and I thanked God for my excellent physical condition. The mud balled up on my combat boots and I felt like I had heavy weights on my feet as I ran.

The squad got across the field without anyone being hit, either by our own fire or the German fire, and started searching through the little strip of woods for the Germans, yelling all the while for them to come out and surrender. We found a total of five Germans all together and they were all pretty well shot up. One of the Germans had been shot five times.

We waited in the woods with our prisoners for a while and finally got orders for our squad to move up to the crest of the hill that overlooked the German positions. As we crawled up to the top of the ridge line, we felt pretty scared. There were just ten of us and we were about a quarter of a mile ahead of everyone else. We looked over the crest of the hill and there in a field about three hundred yards in front of us, we saw Germans laying everywhere. They were all sprawled out and looked dead. Lt. Emory told us to fire some shots into them and we did. None of them moved so we figured that by now that they were all dead or pretty badly wounded. Then, far across the field beyond the Germans, we saw a white flag moving out of the woods. We began preparation to fire in that direction before we saw that the flag was being carried by some GI's with two

German prisoners. Then out of the woods came more GI's towards the Germans laying in the field. These GI's were part of another company that had come around the flank to surround the Germans. As this group moved across the field, one by one, most of the Germans that we thought were dead got up and put their hands over their head as a sign of surrender. Only about ten of the group were actually dead. We had captured or killed everyone of them and not a single one had escaped back to the town of Oberkirchen.

We then moved on through the woods for quite a way and came to a place where it sounded as if quite a fight was taking place. However, it was actually only a German ammo dump blowing up. This gave us a scare for a while as the exploding shells whistled around us. It was almost dark, so we were ordered to dig in along side the road and in the woods not far from the dump. It had been raining all day and we were soaked to the bone. The woolen uniforms that we were wearing were wet and rubbing the skin raw wherever they touched and I was perfectly miserable.

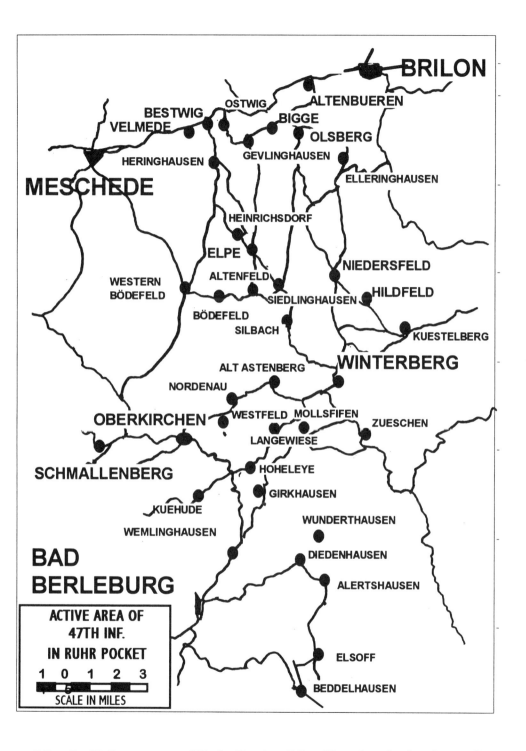

Map 7 - Enlargement of Ruhr Region Map Showing Active Area of 47th Infantry

103

Chapter 11

The Approach to Oberkirchen
(April 2-3)

It was well after dark before we got our holes dug and the rain was still pouring down. We covered the holes with our ponchos and some logs. The water still poured through and I spent the most miserable night of my life in that hole. The ammunition dump was still blowing up across the road, and in addition, the German artillery was firing at us. I woke up every ten minutes and each time I did the shells seemed to be coming in right around us and the shrapnel sounded as if it was heading right for us. The water started filling up the hole that I shared with Lazurus. Once during the night, Lazarus had to leave the hole to relieve himself and when he came back he said that he could hear Germans talking all around us. We decided that on a night like this they would never find us unless they fell into our holes. Even though the water was coming into the hole, my body managed to warm it up so long as I didn't move. When I had to leave the hole myself, I was never able to warm the water in the hole again and I nearly froze. I didn't hear any Germans when I got up, so I figured that Lazurus must have been imagining things, although I wouldn't have been surprised at anything that went on that night.

Tuesday, April 3

The next morning when we got up, we found that we had about three inches of water in our holes and we were soaked to the bone. The rain was still pouring down. The cooks sent up some C rations in a pot of hot water and some hot coffee. This was as close as they could get to supplying us hot food. Our blankets were soaked and weighed about ten pounds [81] so the supply people took them up and

---

[81] Most of us had been issued sleeping bags before we joined the unit, but we soon got rid of them in favor of a single blanket, which was much more practical

said that they would bring us some dry ones later in the day. The hot C Rations and coffee tasted mighty good and they warmed us up a little before we moved out through the woods and into the mountainous terrain. Brushing against the wet fir trees kept us soaked to the bone. All the time we could hear what we supposed were our tanks moving along the road below us.

We met only a little resistance and, after climbing some very high hills and going through some very thick forests, we came to a hill where we could look down and see the road that our tanks were supposed to move up with F Company. We could hear and see tanks near the road but they were not ours. There were three German tanks moving around in a field and since we had an artillery liaison officer with us, our artillery was trying their best to hit them. However, they were moving around so fast that our artillery was not able to zero in on them. The tanks finally moved off down the road and around a bend.

We moved on up to the top of the hill where we found a woodsman's shack. There were three Frenchmen in the shack and we shot it up pretty good before we knew that they were French. The only damage from the shooting was to a horse that was hitched to a wagon on one side of the shack. The horse was wounded pretty badly so Captain Petty had someone put it out of its misery. Captain Petty loved horses and he hated to see it destroyed. E Company was immediately spread out around the top of hill, but before we could start digging our holes Captain Petty moved out with the 1st and 3rd Platoons across a wide open field to attack the little crossroads town of Oberkirchen. The 2nd and 4th Platoons were left to hold down the flank of the battalion on top of the hill, which was the highest ground in the area. The 4th Platoon and the heavy weapons machine gunners set up their guns to cover the men as they attacked.

---

for a combat soldier. You could cover yourself with the blanket when you road on trucks and tanks and a blanket was much more practical for use in a fox-hole.

The attack was to start at one o'clock under the cover of smoke. The artillery couldn't hit close enough on the other side of the hill to lay the smoke in front of the town so it was left to the heavy mortars of the heavy weapons company to provide the support. The heavy mortars were dug in just below us on the backside of the hill and they threw in hundreds of white phosphorus shells.

Before long, the whole town was on fire. While the rest of the company went into town, the 2nd and 4th Platoons watched from the hill. The attacking elements managed to get in to town fairly easy, losing only two or three men in the attack. One man was shot in the stomach as they crossed the field and we heard that he later died. As the company entered town, six German tanks moved out from a road on the other side of town and all kinds of German trucks and vehicles started leaving the town. From our position, high up on the hill, we could see the entire town and all of the roads that led into it. Our machine guns on the hill were firing on the vehicles and although they were almost a mile away they were making them move along. During much of this time, I was standing beside and talking to the artillery liaison officer[82] as he directed the artillery fire.

Also, during this time, I was trying to dig my hole and keep watching the town at the same time. I had just gotten my hole dug when the clouds lifted a bit and I heard some of our planes (P-47's) come in and start strafing the town. They dropped their bombs right in the center of town. All kinds of German fire came up at them and we were amazed that so much fire could be thrown up from that one little town. We were concerned that the planes were bombing our own positions and I asked the lieutenant where the company was located at that time. He said that the last time he had talked to Capt. Petty, he was just across the street from where the bombs had hit. Pretty soon we saw what had happened. There were still about ten German tanks hiding in the town and the planes had attacked these

---

[82]Forty-eight years later I found out that this officer was Lt. Pete Rice of the 84th Field Artillery.

tanks. We were worried about Captain Petty for awhile, but we soon found out that he was OK.

After the bombing, the tanks started fleeing town and our mortars hit one as it went up the road. We could see a ball of flame spurt up from the back of the tank when the shell hit. The tank stopped and a German jumped off and ran for a house across the road.   Then the tank started off down the road again and then another shell hit it and it stopped once more. This time some more Germans jumped off and ran for the house and once again the tank started up and moved off down the road. This time it kept going on around a bend and behind a hill. The artillery and mortars were ripping up everything but didn't seem to be hurting any of the German tanks. All of the tanks made it out of town OK. Our planes came in again and although we couldn't see them from where we were, we were told that they knocked out three of the tanks on further up the road. By now it looked like the whole town of Oberkirchen was on fire. The bombs had started a big fire in the center of town and the smoke (white phosphorus) shells that hit the houses had also started fires.

It was still raining off and on and now it was also sleeting and snowing. Since our blankets had been turned in, we had nothing to sleep under that night. Hamlet and I had dug our holes together. Around dark, I came back from the shack and had just gotten into the hole to rest, when the Germans started shelling us. About nine large shells came into our positions in about five minutes. When I went back to the shack the next time, I saw that all nine shells had hit between my hole and the shack and had left craters as big as those usually caused by bombs. Luckily, although they knocked down all the trees around us and made huge craters, no one was even shook up by the shelling. Some of the shells had landed only about ten feet from some of our foxholes. Obviously, the Germans knew that we were on the hill. They were probably trying to either hit the shack or the machine guns and mortars that were firing at them.

Right after the shelling, Lt. Emory told Hamlet and I to go up to the very top of the hill just above the shack and dig our hole there for the night. By now it was pitch dark and impossible to see anything. Digging a decent hole under such conditions was just about impossible. Two of the fellows had already dug a hole a few feet away on the hilltop, so rather than to trying to dig in the dark, Hamlet and I proposed to them that we take turns staying in the one hole on the hill during the night. The other guys were already comfortable in their hole and weren't interested in taking turns at guard duty. It was so wet and cold that night, and since we didn't have any blankets, Hamlet and I decided that we wouldn't attempt to start another hole in the dark. So we wandered back in the pitch black night and got our equipment from our old holes. On the way we fell in one shell hole after another and nearly broke our necks on the fallen trees. But we got our stuff and then went back the same way that we had come, falling in the same holes as we went. It was so dark that I was holding on to Hamlet's hand and once, when I let it go, I had to call out to him before I finally got hold of his hand again.

The bottom of the little shack was full of men, mostly from our heavy weapons platoon(4th) and H Company, the battalion heavy weapons company. They had their machine guns set up along the rim of the woods looking down the hill. Hamlet and I decided that we would sleep up above in the hay loft of the shack. We got up into the loft and I went to sleep right away. I woke up about an hour later and I felt like I was freezing. I decided to go down below to where the machine gunners were sleeping and where there had once been a fire. Hamlet was sleeping soundly so I didn't disturb him. The room down below was full of sleeping men, so I just sort of nudged my way in between some of them to get warm. I finished the night on the dirt floor snuggled in with the some grumbling machine gunners and managed to get a little sleep.

The next morning I got up bright and early and went out to the part of the hole that we had dug the night before. I started standing guard so that the Lieutenant would think that I had been there all night instead of in the shack. The scheme worked and we got some more fellows to stand guard with us out there during the day and managed to enlarge our hole[83] so we would be able to stay in it the next night.

Early that morning, some of the men from the 1st and 3rd Platoons wandered into our positions from the town. They said that they had been cut off from the rest of the men in the company and that the only way they could get back to the unit was to come around to where we were. They said that the Germans had slipped through and got in behind them during the night. It was not until later that we heard the complete story of what was really happening in the town.

---

[83] A fox-hole was the warmest and safest place to stay, so we were very pleased to finally get one dug in the right place.

Chapter 12

The Battle For Oberkirchen
(April 3-6)

We had eaten our last rations the night before, and, besides being cold and miserable, we didn't have a thing to eat this morning. We knew that there was no way in the world that a jeep could get to us with hot food. Lt. Emory took off down the steep hill towards where the heavy mortars were set up to see if he could get some C rations from them. He knew that the heavy weapons companies usually had vehicles attached to them for handling ammo and probably would be carrying extra rations. They were on the opposite side of the hill from the town of Oberkirchen and were firing over the hill at the town.

Lt. Emory managed to get some rations, but he didn't get enough for the whole platoon, so we had to divide them up among all of us. Some of the fellows still had rations that they had been carrying so we put all of the rations together and managed to have at least one ration for each one of us. There was also some zwieback bread and preserves in barrels on the wagon that the horse had been pulling, so we unpacked and ate some of that.

It wasn't until late that night that we managed to get some food from the company kitchen. There had been food started up to us the night before. However, while the jeep was stopped in front of the E Company CP in Oberkirchen, the Germans had shot the guard, fired a Panzer Faust through the door of the CP killing the radio operator[84] and a German civilian, and stole the jeep with all the food. Unknown to us at the time, we were cut off from the rest of the 9th

---

[84]Pfc. Walter F. McLhinney, one of the veterans still left with the company. McLhinney had joined the unit in England and had been wounded three times during the fighting in France and Germany.

Division. The 39th Infantry Regiment had been forced to come along behind us and clear out the Germans in order that the rest of the division could reach us.

I spent most of the day in the shack trying to keep a little warm and then, late in the afternoon, Hamlet and I went out to prepare a really good hole for the night. We dug it good and deep and made it plenty big. Then we got some old iron beds out of the shack and laid them over the top of the hole to hold up the boards that we laid over it. Then we piled about six inches of dirt over the top just leaving an opening at one end where we could get in and out. We then lined the hole with plenty of the hay that was in the shack. The typical infantryman was always talking and dreaming of having a fur lined foxhole. We now had about as close to a fur lined foxhole as you could get.[85]

During the day (April 4th), the Germans had made many counterattacks[86] in the town of Oberkirchen and these counterattacks were supported by tanks. One of our tankers said that when the Germans had left the town the night before they must have thought they had knocked out all of our armor. The next morning they sent in three light Mark III tanks right down the main street. Our tanks were waiting for them and they knocked out the first tank right away and after that, the other two fled. During the day, the Germans sent in Mark V and Mark VI tanks and the tankers were also able to knockout one of them. The tanker said that they had their gun trained on the corner of the street and they saw the German tank

---

[85]35 years after the battle of Oberkirchen I visited the site on top of the hill where we had been dug in. My foxhole was still there, right on the very top of the hill, albeit the bed spring top was gone. The little hut where we had tried to keep warm was also still there, looking as bleak as ever.

[86]A description of the fighting at Oberkirchen is given in the Distinguished Unit Citation presented to the 2nd Battalion for the action at Oberkirchen. A copy of this citation is given in the Appendix.

stick its nose gun around the corner. They had their gun ready to fire but the German tank waited there a long time. The tankers said that they were ready to fall over from tenseness. But the German tank finally moved, and our tank hit him twice, right in the side, knocking him out. Another tank was knocked out by Captain Petty. He threw a smoke grenade into the tank after he had hit it with a Panzer Faust.[87] The Germans still didn't come out, so he threw a fragmentation grenade into the tank and silenced it for good. We lost one of our own tanks and one of the tank destroyers was abandoned when the Germans pinned it down and made its position untenable. The TD was later recovered and put back into service.

On the hill where we were, shells whizzed over our heads constantly, but the Germans kept trying to knock out our mortars behind the hill. That night we finally got chow. We had to carry it about a mile from the jeep to the top of the hill before we could eat. Supply also sent up two blankets a piece, which really helped us out during the cold nights. That night we slept very well.

The next day (April 5th), we were supposed to be relieved by the 99th Division. We went down the hill at about ten o'clock in the morning to rejoin the company. Before we went down, I walked over to the crest of the hill and watched a violent tank battle that was taking place in the field in front of us. There were four American tanks in the field firing over a slight rise in ground at some German tanks in the woods. The German tanks were firing back at the American tanks and quite a fight seemed to be going on. This was the first time that I had been able to stand back at a distance and watch our tanks shoot it out with German tanks. Our tanks moved on out across the field so I suppose the German tanks retired from the action.

---

[87]The Panzer Faust was an ideal weapon for fighting in towns such as Oberkirchen and it was used extensively by both sides.

We pulled back down the road and waited for transportation to come pick us up. Several shells hit close by as we waited, but they did no damage. We finally got onto armored halftrack personnel carriers[88], and just as we did, it started raining again. We waited inside the halftracks and didn't get orders to move out till four o'clock that afternoon. Just as we were leaving, we saw a barrage of shells hit the hill where we had been. The whole hill looked like it was going up in smoke. We had just gotten away from that place in the nick of time. We heard later that the Germans retook the hill and flanked the town of Oberkirchen and that the 99th Division briefly lost the town to the Germans. All the time that we had been on the hill, the 2nd Battalion had been without any other flank protection. The 2nd and 4th platoons, with attachments from H Company, had provided the only protection from German attack in that direction.

The 2nd Battalion was awarded the Presidential Unit Citation (Distinguished Unit Citation), the highest award for combat units, for its part in the fighting at Oberkirchen (See Appendix B) and E Company, the unit that had only two weeks before had been completely decimated by the fighting at Remagen, had become a veteran fighting unit again and had stood up to the best that the Germans could offer. In combat, it doesn't take long to learn when there is good leadership available. The action of E Company was cited in the Presidential Citation [89] awarded to the 2nd Battalion..

The battalion rode about twenty-five kilometers on the halftracks to the town of Winterberg. Winterberg, before the war, had been a sports resort and winter playground. In fact, part of the Winter Olympics of 1936 had been held here at Winterberg. There were

---

[88]This was the Personnel Carrier M3 which was driven by a 147hp White engine and could reach a maximum speed of 45mph. It contained a .50cal machine gun mounted on a pedestal and seats for ten men. These halftracks were the basic transport for armored infantry squads but were not assigned as transport to the Infantry Division Rifle Companies. The halftracks used here at Oberkircken would have been borrowed from some other unit.

[89]See Appendix B for the text of the citation.

many resort type apartments and dormitories for skiers and we found stacks of skis in all of these houses. The town was also a key road junction and had been pretty well beaten up during recent fighting, but we were able to find a nice apartment to stay in. We were really glad to get inside once again after sleeping outside in the terrible weather of the past week.

Our joy was short lived. At about eleven that night, we got the order to saddle up, and we moved out again into the pitch black night. As we left the blacked out buildings, we had to hold onto each other to keep from getting lost in the dark. We found the halftracks and got onto them again. The halftracks moved out of town and proceeded to drive along the roads under completely blacked out conditions with no lights. Some one must have wanted us to move awfully bad to have brought us out on the roads under these conditions. We managed to stay on the road until about four in the morning. At that time our driver lost the road completely and our half-track ran off into a ditch. We were completely stuck in the ditch so we had to wait until morning to get the halftrack out of it. While we waited for daylight, we went across to a farm house. The people in the house treated us well and we were able to stay warm by a fire in the kitchen. A tank pulled up a short time later to wait with us. The tank had run out of gasoline and gotten lost from the convoy so he had decided to wait till morning and go in with us. As soon as daylight came, the tank found some gas and pulled us out of the ditch, and we started down the road again with the tank following along behind us. Somewhere along the way we lost the tank again, but we kept on going and, with the help of MP's stationed at each crossroads, finally caught up with the rest of the convoy outside of Brilon.

In Brilon, we found a fairly good place to stay in a private house. That day at lunch, it was arranged for us to eat with the 1st Division, who were also in the town. So we got some good hot food for a change. We had to move to a school house that afternoon and we stayed in the schoolhouse that night. That afternoon Hamlet and I went over to the aid station to see if we could get our feet and arms treated. We each had sores all over them from wearing wet shoes and wet clothes for so long. Evidently Hamlet's problems were much worse than mine because the medics had him evacuated to the hospital for trench foot. I got myself doctored up for cuts on my arm and raw places that the wool had rubbed on my hands and arms and behind my knees. I also got my heels taped up where they had been bothering me. I couldn't help but wonder if the night that I had let Hamlet stay in that cold barn loft might have aggravated his condition. After all, we had been fighting side by side and sleeping in the same holes for a month. Something must have happened to make his condition worse than mine. I never saw Hamlet again after that. He never returned to the unit as far as I know.

Some of the guys asked Hart to cut their hair that night. Hart was a pretty good barber and usually in demand. There was a pair of clippers somewhere in the company that he used when he cut hair. I didn't get my hair cut that night because Hart was so busy with the others.

That day, several us had been popping off to each other about how inexperienced Lt. Emory was and the foolish things that he sometimes made us do. We looked up and he was standing there just behind us. He had heard it all, but he just grinned and made no comment. That night in the schoolhouse, the squad bedded down all in a row in one of the rooms. Lt. Emory put his blanket down beside us and slept with us

Chapter 13

Toward Ostwig and the Ruhr River
(April 7)

The next morning, April 7, we moved out bright and early to Oldsberg, where we stayed until about noon. We had thought we would be in Oldsberg for the rest of the day and the kitchen set up to cook steaks for supper. We all lay around in the back of a building and wrote letters to the folks back home. It seemed that everyone in the platoon thought that it was necessary to write letters home that afternoon. It seemed a strange time to write since we usually wrote the few letters that we wrote in the evening. Never-the-less I wrote some letters home myself. I had just received a letter from my mother telling me that my younger brother, Clint, was trying to enlist in the Navy. I wrote a letter urging Clint not to volunteer for anything before it was absolutely necessary. I told him that it was impossible to describe the horrors of war, but I could assure him that war was not very glamorous and that he would want no part of it.

To our surprise, shortly after noon we were called out and told to mount the tanks. We moved out on the tanks through the town of Bigge and into the little town of Gevlinghausen, which had been taken by the 3rd Battalion that morning. It was cold riding on the tanks. I had a civilian blanket that I had picked up somewhere along the way and Sgt. Elmer R. Stewart, one of the squad leaders, and I huddled together under the blanket as we rode along on the tank. One of the nice things about riding on a tank was the fact that the tanks engines and exhaust usually provided us with some warmth, but today the cold wind was biting if you didn't have something to cover with.

We got off the tanks at Gevlinghausen and moved into some houses on the edge of town and waited for awhile. Some of the men found some potato alcohol and drank it while we waited[90]. I had latched on to a package of powdered chocolate drink so I mixed it with some water from my canteen and drank it while I waited. This powder made a delicious chocolate drink and, since it had a powdered milk base, it could be mixed with plain water. The chocolate drink was not provided in our regular rations but came in the Ten-In-One rations that the tankers carried. So we had to bum it off of them whenever we could. Most tankers were pretty good about letting the infantryman have just about anything they had and they were usually well supplied since they could carry so much on the back of the tanks. We infantrymen were the beggars of the army since we had to carry everything on our backs and we usually didn't have very much with us.

In a short time, the company was called out and began advancing into some deep woods just on the edge of town. We had just moved into the woods when the front of the company was pinned down in a little ditch by small arms fire and the officers moved us all up on a line. A few of the men that had been drinking the alcohol were drunk by now and began shouting and running back to the rear when the shooting began.

Lt. Emory took one squad around to flank the Germans. Sgt. Stewart, the squad leader, and Lum, the first scout of this squad were shot immediately. The Lieutenant came back and took my squad and the other squad up out of the ditch to charge the Germans. Our charge didn't get far before we were also pinned down by the German fire. I kept running forward and managed to get into an old sunken road bed that provided a little protection. I heard Lt. Emory coming up behind me yelling for a medic for the men that had been shot. I turned to look in his direction and, just as I did, he was

---

[90] This was highly unusual. I remember no other instance when the men in the 2nd Platoon actually drank intoxicating beverages during the time they were advancing or fighting. Most of the time, the alcohol (if any were found) would have been drunk at night and its effect would have been gone by morning.

118

hit by a bullet and fell backwards into a small bush a few feet away from me along the other side of the sunken road.

Bullets kept hitting the ground all around us. Some of them seemed to be a type of explosive bullet that popped when they hit the ground. I had a Panzer Faust with me and I kept trying to shove it as far away from me as possible, for fear that some stray bullet might hit it and cause it to detonate. I could see Hart on the ridge just above me firing away with his BAR, not seeming to even notice the bullets that were flying all around us. This was the worst fire fight that I had ever experienced but I can truly say that I was too busy fighting for my life to really be afraid. We were trying to fight back as best we could without having the slightest idea where the enemy was located or where the firing was coming from.

One fork of the road bed that I was laying in led down the hill to a building which was about thirty yards in front of us. In fact, there were two buildings and a shed in the group. When the lieutenant had been shot, I thought that the firing had come from one of these buildings, so I kept firing bullets into every window to keep anyone from firing out. I couldn't see the bullets breaking any glass in the windows and I wondered if I was doing any good at all. I didn't give any thought to the fact that the windows may not have ever had any glass in them.[91]

I was laying on the side of the incline, and I couldn't fire with my right hand because I had to use it to keep myself balanced. The thought flashed through my mind that back in basic training they had told us that you couldn't fire an M-1 rifle with your left hand. I also remembered that they had said that you should never get your hand in the way of the operating rod or it would tear your thumb off. All of this ran through my mind as I kept on firing with my left hand and thinking how wrong they had been in basic. Practically every time I

---

[91] These buildings, although dilapidated, were still standing when I visited the sight in 1994. The scars from our bullets still show in the wooden siding but there is no glass in the windows in the upper part of the large building.

fired, the rod came back and hit my hand with no noticeable damage. I was too excited to notice any pain.

Finally, the firing slowed down and what was left of our squad went down to clear the buildings. I threw a grenade into one of the sheds before we charged it, but there were no soldiers in the buildings. We did find some civilians hiding in one of the sheds. One of the men who could speak English came up and shook our hands and said, "We have been waiting for you to come". He seemed very glad to see us. The group of buildings appeared to be an old mill and across the road from the buildings was a small stream that we were to learn later was one of the sources of the Ruhr River. The fabulous Ruhr that we had read about in our geography books and heard so much about in the news, did not look very impressive to us. It was only about ten or fifteen feet wide at this point.

During this whole engagement, none of us had seen where the shots were coming from. People were dropping all around us and we had no idea which way to fight back. This was the terrible part of fighting in a wooded area. You have no idea where the enemy might be or which way to fire when the shooting begins. After the battle was over, we saw no Germans, and we never found out where they came from or where they went.[92]

The medics came and started working on Lt. Emory. He was still propped up by small bush in a half sitting position. He remained conscious and was talking to some of the officers, even though the bullet that hit him had passed all the way through his chest and body. I went on up the hill with the rest of my squad and joined the remainder of the platoon. During the battle, the dry grass on the

---

[92]When I visited this sight thirty five years later, I was still perplexed by the question of where had the German fire come from. At that time, I found what appeared to be a German defensive position in the edge of the sunken road just a little ahead of where Lt. Emory was shot. If the Germans were firing from this position, it would account for Lt. Emory being shot as he came up the sunken road and the other people being killed in the woods above the road.

ground under the trees had started to burn and the whole hillside was now smoldering. I saw one fellow laying face down in the smoldering grass, obviously dead. I asked one of the other fellows who the dead man was and he said that it was PFC Jerry M. Lum, a Chinese boy who had been first scout in the second squad. I couldn't help but recall that Hart had cut Lum's hair the night before when we had a few minutes of relaxation.

The platoon moved out through the woods again, but no one fired at us this time. We were still jumpy from our experience on the hillside so we kept behind trees as much as we could. We would run a short distance and then drop behind a tree. By doing this, we felt that the Germans would not have time to get off a good shot at us before we dropped behind cover again.

I came to a barbed wire obstacle of the type that was spread on the battlefield to impede progress. Usually these are placed in front of enemy fortifications and are covered by machine guns and other weapons. I managed to get over the wire with no problem, but all the time that I was crossing it I was expecting to either be shot or to set off a mine or booby trap. We finally fought our way on through the woods to the bottom of a high stone hill. On top of the hill was a big tower similar to the ones you find on the old castles around Germany.

There were a large number of French people in an old mine at the foot of the hill. We sent them back to the rear and just as we did, a German car came roaring down the road below us. Although we fired at the car, it went on passed us. We knew that it couldn't get far up the road so we sent Dawson, our bazooka man, down the hill to knock it out if it came back. Just as we expected, it did come back. Dawson fired and hit the car, knocking it around and off the road. Neither of the two Germans in the car appeared to be hurt and they jumped out and started to run. Some of the boys nearby captured one of them and told him that they would shoot him if he didn't call the other one back. This brought the other one back and we sent them both to the rear as prisoners.

After much climbing, we finally got to the top of the stone hill and cleared the Germans out of the tower. We stopped for a minute, and I stood my rifle against a rock and started to eat part of a ration. As I looked over the crest of the hill, there in the rocks just below me about thirty or forty yards away, was a German officer walking around as if he owned the place and evidently trying to get away. I yelled to Hart, who was right beside me, and as soon as we could get our rifles to our shoulders, we both started firing. We reacted too late and the German dived into a crevice in the rocks before we could hit him.. Hart and I yelled to some of the platoon on up the hill to let them know that he was coming their way and they caught him without much trouble.

As we stood and looked off the hill, we saw a fairly large town (Ostwig) lying in the valley about a mile in front of us. From where we stood, it appeared that all we had to do was go down the hill and the town would be ours. The town stretched along the Ruhr River as far as we could see (we were actually looking at several towns, the largest of which was Bestwig). We began directing mortar fire into the town and watching the shells hit the buildings. Captain Petty noticed someone walking around on the ground some distance down below us and he asked me to hand him my rifle so that he could shoot him. I could see that the person in the distance was a GI and I told Captain Petty that this was the case. However, Capt. Petty insisted that no one was supposed to be down in that area and that the man should be shot. It was all that I could do to talk him out of taking a shot. I did finally convince him not to shoot and by then it was time for us to attack the town down below.

For the attack on the town, it was originally planned that F Company would ride into town on a company of tanks. However, the tanks were held up by a road block that was back down the road in the direction from which we had come. Twilight was beginning so, at around seven o'clock that night, E Company was ordered into the town. With H Company covering us from the hill with their machine guns, we moved down to the road and proceeded into the town.

Again I was amazed at how incredibly fast an infantry company can move through a town. In fact, sometimes it seemed that we outran ourselves. My squad was assigned one side of the street but as we kept moving up, the buildings were being cleared so fast that we couldn't find buildings that hadn't already been cleared. When your clearing a town, you run as fast as you possibly can from building to building, trying to get from one covered area to the next before the Germans can get a good shot at you. Quickness is the only protection that you have.

That day, about half way through the town, our tanks came roaring down one of the streets at top speed. They had their sirens blaring and at first, we all thought that they were German tanks. We almost panicked, but one of the officers yelled over for us to keep moving, that these were our own tanks. These were the company of tanks, along with F Company, that had been held up by the road block.

So far, I had been able to move from one house to the next and keep pretty well under cover. But now I came to a street that I had to cross. We were at an open place along the road where there were no houses and I could hear the bullets whining back and forth across the open place. I darted across as fast as I could, and fortunately I managed to get across without being hit.

Our squad then moved across to another house where we couldn't get the doors open. I ran around to a big window in front and broke in the window. When I did, the whole window frame fell down on top of me. It was quite a crash and I thought that I had finally gotten the *million dollar wound*.[93] To my amazement, my only injury was a

---

[93]Every GI was looking for the wound that didn't hurt very much but would get him evacuated to the hospital for a long time.

few cuts on my wrists. Well, at least after that we all got into the house pretty fast, but we found no Germans there. I had to go through the same procedure in several more of the houses that we entered because all of the people in this town had locked their doors. Many times, if there were civilians inside and they heard us trying to get in, they would run up out of the cellar and open the door for us.

At one time during the attack on this town, we ran into some of the black soldiers from F Company's 5th Platoon. They had probably come in with the tanks when the tanks had attacked the town. The black soldiers were great fighters and seemed to take to the attack with great enthusiasm. They had a reputation of expending a lot of ammunition and really shooting a place up when they attacked. They were a colorful bunch of guys and we got a big kick out of being associated with them.[94] They always seemed to show up somewhere where you least expected to find them.

We finally got to the end of the area that we were supposed to clear, and we stopped and were assigned a house for the night. By now it was well after dark, but the whole town was burning and there was plenty of light. There was a terrific tank battle going on over in another part of town. We could hear the tanks firing their high velocity shells at a rapid clip.

We caught our breath a little while and went down to the river (this was the same little river that we had seen earlier running beside the mill) and filled our canteens. We had not had any water brought to us and we had drunk a lot that day. The water tasted good even though it came out of the river. The medics would have raised the dickens if they had known we were drinking the raw river water, but by then we were desperately thirsty.

---

[94] Fifty years later, Capt. Ray Schmader, Commander of F Company in 1945, remembered the black infantrymen as being very good soldiers. He recalled that most of the group that he had were very intelligent and well educated.

We didn't get to rest long because Lt. Kenny, the company executive officer, came over and took our platoon to a tank commander and we were attached to them for the night. All we did after being attached to the tanks was to go over to a huge mansion, or castle like building, to spend the night. We pulled guard that night with the tankers to give them some infantry support in case of an attack.

The house was so big that Hart and I wandered off from the rest of the squad and found a great big room and bed and slept in it that night. Before we went to bed, we went back to see where the rest of the squad was sleeping and found all of them, side by side, in one big bed just like the *seven dwarfs*. They all got a big kick out of sleeping in a bed so big that the whole squad could sleep in it. That night, the house was so big, we could all have had separate rooms if we had wanted them. But there is always comfort and safety in numbers. The night went by quietly enough and the next morning we went back and joined the company.

Chapter 14

Along the Ruhr
(April 8)

It was not until now that we found out the extent of the casualties from the day before. There had been about thirty-three men in our platoon when we started out the day before and now there were only nineteen of us left. We got a few replacements this morning and some of the men that were missing showed up later. The missing men had been wandering in the woods in a daze from shock and fear since the day before. There were five dead that did not come back and two that were wounded so badly that they never returned to combat. Because our platoon had been hit so hard and had lost some of its leaders, we eliminated the third squad and went back to two squads again.

Lt. Kenny came up in the morning and gave us as much information as he knew. We all felt like orphans now without a platoon leader. Lt. Kenny said that Lt. Emory had been evacuated to the rear and he thought that he would live, even though his wound was pretty bad. Lt. Kenny also told us that Sgt. Stewart had been killed and he asked us not to tell Sgt. Shivers, one of the other squad leaders, that Stewart was dead. Shivers and Stewart had been buddies since their training days back in Texas and Shivers was already a nervous wreck. Lt. Kenny didn't think that Shivers could stand the shock of Stewart's death. So we all told Shivers that Stewart had been slightly wounded and taken back to the hospital. Several other members of our platoon were missing including Mace, and a jolly little fat guy from West Virginia named Riley. Lt. Kenny[95] also told us that our supper from the night before was coming up and that we would get to have steaks after all, even if they were a little cold.

---

[95] Shortly after this, Lt. Kenny moved to G Company to become its commander.

Later that morning, Mace returned to the platoon. He told a very frightening story of having been pinned down on the hill with Sgt. Stewart and being afraid to move. He lay on the hill acting dead until after dark and he was sure the Germans were gone. Some of the survivors that had been nearby also told the story of how Finnegan had try to crawl forward under fire and pull Lum back to safety. Finnegan was from Boston and had been a Chaplains assistance until he came to the 2nd Platoon. In all appearances until this time, he acted as if he were a notorious coward and no one wanted to be near him during the fighting.

At about one o'clock in the afternoon, we started out down the highway and over into the next town. The towns along the Ruhr were situated one right after the other so you could not tell when you left one town and entered another. There were huge railroad yards and factories in this town and some of the facilities had been left burning by the tanks. We saw dead German soldiers all along the road. We were now part of Task Force Birks[96] and had the 32nd Cavalry and 16th Cavalry in front of us. Their new light tanks were eating up the German resistance. This was the first time that we had seen these new light tanks[97] that were assigned to cavalry and reconnaissance units and we were impressed by them. We entered the town of Velmede and then went out to the outskirts to guard the flanks. No one had cleared the big wooded hills on each side of the town.[98]

---

[96]Task forces were usually named for the General or officer who commanded them. This one was commanded by Brigadier General Hammond D. Birks, the assistant Division commander of the 9th Division. It consisted of the 47th Infantry and elements of the 7th Armored Division and 32nd Calvary Squadron.
[97]This was the 18 ton M24 Chaffee tank which mounted a 75 mm gun on its turret.
[98]This was typical of armored warfare where the tanks moved quickly down the roads, often bypassing large pockets of Germans in the hills and woods away from the roads.

We spent the rest of the day there on the outskirts of Velmede relaxing and waiting for our next mission. Once, during the afternoon, a German soldier came in and said that he had a comrade out in the woods that had been wounded. He wanted us to come out and get him and bring him in so that they could surrender. The platoon sergeant sent two of us out to see what was up. The German led us about a mile up into the woods on the hill and we finally came to the wounded German. He was shot up so badly that he was unconscious.

We decided that it would be best to get some help to move the badly wounded man so I sent the other GI back into the town to get some civilians to carry the wounded man back. Meanwhile I remained there in the woods guarding the two Germans. I spoke in my broken German to the soldier that had led me out to this spot and tried to find out what had happened. The German told me that their officers had shot both of them when they had wanted to surrender. The man that I was talking to was shot in the leg himself and he said that the rest of the unit had retreated back into the woods after the officers had shot him and his buddy. I was kind of uneasy out there all by myself waiting for the other fellow to return. I was afraid that this might be some kind of a trap set by the Germans. However, it was very quiet in the woods and nothing out of the way happened. After about forty-five minutes, the other GI came back with a drove of civilians and they made a litter and carried the wounded man back to town.

That night we had to pull guard with the anti-tank boys. Nothing much happened during the night except that there was a tremendous glow in the air over towards the town of Meschede, where the 3rd Battalion and the cavalry were attacking. The glow lit the night up as if it were day. At that time we were staying in a house with a German lady and her married daughter. The daughter was sobbing all of the time and the mother told us that the girls husband was in the German army and fighting somewhere nearby. They showed us pictures of the soldier but, of course, we hadn't seen him among the prisoners that we had captured.

The next morning (April 9), we found out that the Fifth Infantry Division had moved in during the night to relieve us. So that afternoon we got onto our tanks and went back the way that we had come to a little town along the railroad tracks called Brunskappel. While we were in Brunskappel we occupied some little buildings along the side of a big fish pond in a beautiful park. We found some wire and made some fish hooks and tried our hand at fishing in the pond. We thoroughly enjoyed our stay in Brunskappel, where we fished and lay around in the sunshine and took a big long rest.

After the third day (April 11) at Brunskappel, we were given orders to move out. At this time, the 1st and 2nd Battalions of the 47th Infantry were made part of a combat team attached to General Collins VII Corps. We traveled one hundred and twenty five miles that day, crossing the Wesser River at a small town. We went on past Nordheim and then we stopped just to the north of Nordhausen for the night. At Nordhausen, the 3rd Battalion of the 47th Infantry, joined elements of the 3rd Armored Division for the race toward Berlin.

During the day we began to meet something that we had not seen before. Hundreds of ex-prisoners from the Nazi concentration camps. They were the most pathetic sight that any of us had ever seen. The skin seemed to hang from their bones and their heads were shaved and looked like skulls with skin stretched tightly over it. Their eyes seemed huge as they peered out of the sockets in the skull. We gave them food and cigarettes and everything that we could spare. A great lump came into my throat and tears came to my eyes as I looked at this sight. These people were all dressed in the ragged striped gray clothes of the prison camps. I had never seen a human being so degraded by another human being as these people were. Most of the prisoners seemed to be Russian, Polish, or Eastern European, and, as terrible as they looked, they were all in

great spirits on having received their freedom.   Some of the GIs
spoke a little Polish and could converse with them in a crude way.
They told us that the Germans had killed 500 of their comrades just
before we had arrived.

The town that we stayed in that night was just a small little country
town named Wolfsberg.   It had been taken at noon that day by the
3rd Armored Division. We were now about one hundred and ten
miles from Berlin and it didn't look like the 3rd Armored was slowing
down for anything.   Axis Sally, in her propaganda broadcasts from
Berlin, was telling us that the white flags were out all the way to
Berlin.   We didn't know exactly what her strategy was in telling us
this.   Perhaps she was wanting us to hurry and beat the Russians to
Berlin.

We stayed in Wolfsberg two nights waiting for the 3rd Armored to
pass through us. Here again I was amazed at the size and strength of
an armored division. I stood by the rode like a small boy at a parade
and gaped as they went speeding by.

On April 13, we moved out early in the morning into the Harz
mountain area to clean out a large pocket of Germans that had been
by-passed by the armored units. At about mid-morning our column
paused in the edge of a small town. Some of the jeeps had broadcast
frequency radios installed in them which were tuned to the Armed
Forces Network (AFN) and the news came over them that President
Franklin D. Roosevelt had died the day before. This was perhaps the
greatest shock that any of us had experienced during the war.
Everyone stood around in stunned silence, many with tears in their
eyes, not believing that it could happen.   Roosevelt was the only
President that most of us had ever known. Now he was gone, just
when the war seemed about to end. This took a lot of the joy out of
our triumphal march across Germany.

We took the next town, Swenda, without a fight and then, as we set
up a defense in it, several German soldiers came riding into town on

motorcycles. We captured everyone of them and then at about three that afternoon, we got onto trucks and moved out. The tanks led the way, firing continuously into the woods alongside the roads. We traveled through about five miles of dense woods and several Germans were shot and captured along the way. We finally came out of the woods into the town of Brietenstein. We rode up to the outskirts of town and got off the trucks and began to take the town. It was a rough place to clear because the houses were spread pretty far apart and we had trouble crossing the openings under fire.

As we moved up one street, I noticed rifle fire coming from a house down one of the side streets. I moved down the side street and cleared the house and silenced the fire. I felt pretty proud of myself for having taken the initiative to clear the street. When I went back to the main street, I met the new sergeant who was now assigned as acting platoon leader. He asked me where I had been and I told him that I had been clearing that street. He started chewing me out and wanted to know who had told me to do that. I asked him since when do you have to be told to clear out houses when you are being fired upon. From that day on, I never had much use for this sergeant. He was a highly decorated non-com that had seen a lot of action, but he always appeared to me to carry a chip on his shoulder and to have a grudge against the entire platoon, especially me. I think he was the only fellow that I ever met in the army with whom I couldn't get along. He certainly didn't inspire the platoon in the same way that Lt. Emory had done. We finally got the town cleared at about the time that darkness set in. By then we had captured a good many Germans and shot up the place quite a bit.

After we had cleared the town, we went back to the first house that we had cleared to get our packs. The house had been hit and I was unable to find the gas mask pouch in which I carried the film for the camera. I lost several rolls of exposed film that were in the pouch. I still had a couple of rolls in another pack, but we had lost a lot pictures. Of course, I didn't know at that time whether they would have been any good if we had been able to develop them.

We spent the night in a civilian house and the next morning, April 14, we were moved over to another part of town to guard against a German counterattack. We stayed in the top of a house all day looking out the big windows with our binoculars at the land in front of us. Nothing much happened except that we watched the civilians haul the dead by on carts to the cemetery, which was right in front of us. Some of the Polish ex-prisoners that were in the town showed us a grave where German SS troopers had shot twenty Poles and buried them. There were plenty of Poles in the town and they were going through the stores and taking every thing they wanted to wear and eat. We felt that they certainly deserved anything that they could get. After all the cruelty that we had seen, we didn't have much sympathy for the Germans. Later that day, the Poles took some of the people out of our unit, to a spot where there were eighteen fresh graves.

That afternoon we were moved out back of the town and into the woods along with a couple of tanks to guard a road junction. This road junction was the only supply route into the town. One of the side roads had been mined with anti-tank mines and we were placed in foxholes to cover the mined area. Shortly after we got into our holes we noticed a horse coming down the mined road. We knew that he would blow himself sky high when he stepped on the mines, so we crouched down in our holes and held our breath. Nothing happened; the horse stepped gingerly through the mines without setting off a single one.

April 15

The unit pulled out of Brietenstien early in the morning and moved on up into a new town that had been taken by some of the other companies. We bypassed a German tank that had been knocked out by our tankers as he had come around a bend in the road. All of the companies of the battalion got together in the next town and boarded tanks and trucks. We started out for the next town, Harzgerode, which was a good distance away. Two companies of the 1st

Battalion were attached to the 2nd Battalion for the attack on Harzgerode. They were to attack the town up another road.

The tanks were now in front of us firing all of the time. The going was slow because the woods were full of German SS troops[99] firing antiaircraft guns at us. The SS troops wore the distinctive sign of the SS, the two lightening bolts, on their uniform so it was not hard to identify who they were. Several times we jumped off the trucks and dove into the ditches when the antiaircraft guns started shooting our way. There were dead Germans laying everywhere along the sides of the road. There was one spot at a little road junction where fifteen or twenty bodies were laying in one small area. We decided that these must be really fanatical Nazis who were going to die rather than surrender or retreat. As we came up the road a little further, we came to our lead tank sitting in the ditch. The Germans had knocked it out with a panzer faust and killed one of the tankers. He was laying face down in the ditch and as I looked at him I recognized him as one of the tankers with whom I had been especially friendly. I had ridden on his tank several times in the past. A sight such as this always made us wonder about our own mortality. Every day the end of the war seemed nearer but everyday another of us was being killed. I couldn't help but wonder how many more of us would die before it all ended.

---

[99] These were elements of the die-hard German Eleventh SS Panzer Army. These select troops were originally supposed to have died defending Berlin but it was decided to send them to the natural fortress area of the Harz Mountains where they could hold out against the allied advance. The two divisions facing the 9th Division were the *Potsdam* and the *Scharnhorst*.

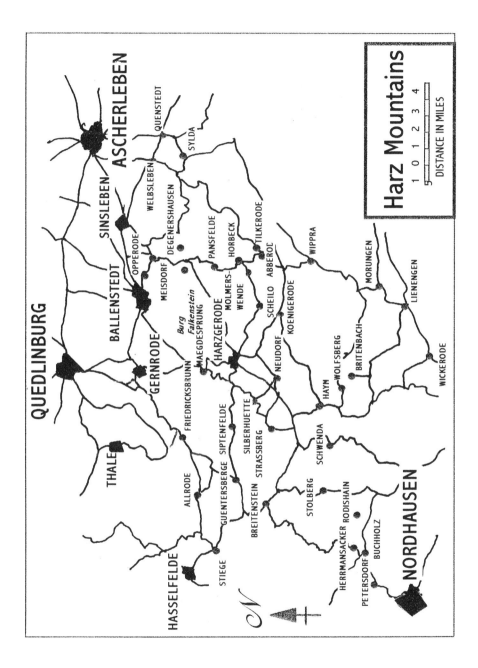

Map 8 - Area of Interest of 47th Infantry in Harz Mountains

Chapter 15

The Harz Mountains
(April 15-17)

We finally had to get off the tanks about two miles form Harzgerode and start out on foot. We had walked about a mile when we passed a couple of cars that the tanks had knocked out a little earlier. There were several high ranking German officers sitting very straight in each of the cars. They were all dead, evidently killed instantly as they drove along. They looked unreal as if they were mannequins in a display case. We learned later that the two companies of the 1st Battalion that were attached to the 2nd Battalion had attacked Harzgerode up another road and had not met much resistance. The Germans had evidently tried to retreat out the other end of town and had run smack into the 2nd Battalion coming up from that direction. This accounted for the heavy resistance that we met.

We got onto the tanks again before we got into town and, when we finally rolled into Harzgerode, we found that the attached elements of the 1st Battalion had beaten us to town and had already cleared it. There were several big fires burning in the town caused by burning oil dumps and other such things. As we entered the town, we ran into some German civilians in the street who were fleeing with all their possessions. They were crying and almost hysterical. I asked one of the German speaking fellows in the platoon what was going on. He said that the German people had seen some of our black soldiers and were terrified by them. They said that Hitler had told them that the black soldiers in the American army were cannibals from Africa who would rape and pillage the towns.

Late that afternoon, who should show up in Harzgerode driving a truck but Riley. He had been missing ever since the battle on the hillside near the old mill. He said that he was now a truck driver for one of the other units. Our officers quickly discovered him and put him back into the 2nd Platoon. Desertion charges were filed against Riley but after the war they were dropped.

We didn't move far into the town that night but stayed over on one side of it. We went to a big apartment house and our platoon stayed in the upstairs part of the house. There were no occupants in the house so we didn't have to move anyone out. However, there was everything in the way of furniture still in the house. That night I had an entire double bed to myself in a private room. We had hot ten-in-one rations for supper and after pulling one hour of guard duty I went to bed.

April 16

The next morning we were up pretty early and after breakfast we moved down to the town square. We were standing right in front of the city hall of the town and there was a dead Polish prisoner laying there on the cobblestone pavement. A shell must have hit him when the town was attacked. For some reason, whenever we ran across a body, we always tried to speculate on how that person had been killed. I guess it was part of our "natural self preservation" training. Or maybe it was just plain curiosity.

The munitions jeep was there passing out ammunition. I got in a heated discussion with the ammo driver when he started to complain about all of the ammunition that we were using. I told him to come up to the front sometime and see for himself where all the ammunition was going.

After picking up the ammo, we were told what we were going to be doing for the day and we started out of town toward our objective. We spread out in the woods and combed them alongside the roads for Germans, but we failed to run across any. The woods didn't last long.   We soon came to their edge and were forced to go across a wide open field toward the next town of Schielo. We came into the town over the crest of a hill. We ran down the hill to the first house and pulled two drunk German soldiers out of it.

We kept on going until we had cleared the town. We took quite a few prisoners, but none of them had guns. While we finished taking this town, the rest of the 2nd Battalion had moved down the highway past E Company and were heading for another town. By the time we caught up with them, they already had the town cleaned out. We paused a little while in the crossroads town of Horbeck while some of our anti-tank guns fired at some Germans in the woods away off to our left. After awhile, we moved down the right fork of the road about two miles and came to two twin towns. One was on the left side of the highway and the other was on the right. E Company was to take the town on the left and F company was to take the one on the right. These were the towns of Abberode and Tilkerode

The town that we were to take was Tilkerode. Once again, we had to cross a small field to get to the town, but this time we moved the tanks up along with the infantrymen in case of trouble. We crawled through a fence and in behind some barns and went into the back of a German house. This way we more or less slipped into the town and caught several German prisoners in the first few houses without firing a shot. As usual, the clearing of the town went extremely fast. During the clearing of a town, everyone is running all of the time. One squad passes you up to clean out the house in front of you and then you pass another up and before you can blink your eyes the town is taken. You can't believe that you have moved as far as you have until you walk back over the distance to get your pack.

At the edge of this town, we came to a German rest center where we captured about a dozen prisoners. There were a couple of officers in the bunch that were captured and they told us that they knew where there were some more Germans. So they led a couple of our boys out to where they were and they brought back about eight more prisoners.

We were all so exhausted that we dropped along side the streets and rested. You can imagine our surprise when a German jeep came driving into town and the Germans got out and surrendered to us. We set machine guns up all along the outskirts of town to guard against a German attack. Shortly after this, about forty more prisoners came in and surrendered in another part of town.

A patrol went out from Tilkerode on a half track to see what was in front of us, but they came back in a hurry when they ran up to within two hundred yards of a German tank. They must have caught the German tank by surprise since he did not fire at them. Our artillery had now spotted the tank and they lay down a barrage all around him before he finally went into the woods.

Just before dark, a tank and another half track with some F Company men on it, went out after the tank. They couldn't find him in the dark, so they were ordered to turn around and come back before he spotted them. I sat on the hill with the commander of F Company [100]and watched the group go out. Finally it got so dark that we couldn't see them anymore and the officer ordered them back. He had communication with the tank through a 300 radio[101].

April 17

We spent a quiet night in Tilkerode and the next morning we moved back out of town in the same direction that we had come, abandoning the town completely. At the town of Horbeck that we had taken the day before, we took the left hand fork in the road this time and started out north. We didn't get far before G Company, which was leading the way, was pinned down by fire from the woods in front of them. They were about a quarter of a mile in front of us, so we could see everything that was happening very clearly.

---

[100] Captain Ray Schmader

[101]The SCR 300 radio was a large FM radio that was carried on the back of the radioman. One of these were provided to each company and the radioman was usually beside the Company Commander during combat action.

The minute that the men dropped in the field, the tanks moved in front to cover them and then stopped and started firing their 76-mm guns as fast as they would go. The tank destroyers that were beside us moved up onto the hill and also started firing their ninety's at the edge of the woods. When the tanks and tank destroyers fired, it looked as if the whole tank had burst into flame. Their guns fired such a high velocity shell that they made more noise than any of the other guns of similar size. The high velocity shells travel on a straight line like a rifle bullet.

The shelling kept up for about half an hour and all of the machine guns on the hill were firing at the woods. Pretty soon, some of the Germans gave up and the rest took off in the other direction. The prisoners told us that there were six German half tracks in the woods with orders to hold us up as long as they could.

We went through the woods and then up over a hill and into the town of Pansfelde. There was no resistance in Pansfelde so we didn't pause in the town but went straight on through town and into some more pine woods on the other side. It was tough going after we got into the woods. We had to fight the German half-tracks at every turn in the road. The day before we had advanced 12,000 meters, or about 7 miles, and captured four towns before noon. Today, we had already gone 5 miles and captured one town before noon.

Chapter 16

Back to Harzgerode
(April 17-22)

There was still a German tank up ahead of us. It was about four in the afternoon before we got to the crossroads at the Gartenhaus of Falkenberg, which was our objective. However, before we captured the crossroads, the 2nd Platoon was sent down through the woods in order to circle around the crossroads. When we did, we ran smack into one of the German armored vehicles. PFC Claud C. Carter, the first scout of our leading squad was just ready to step through a fence when the Germans fired at him with their forty mm gun and killed him instantly. I was only a short distance behind Carter when I heard the German gun fire. After that the German machine guns began to fire at us with their characteristic whine of bullets. The Germans kept firing but we scampered back into the woods and called for mortar fire on the German positions. The Germans soon had to withdraw and we slipped out of the woods, crossed the road, and continued to circle around the crossroads. I didn't know until later that Carter[102] had been killed.

I felt terrible about the death of Carter. I had only know him a short time but I had liked him very much. He was one of the old timers that had been wounded during the battle for the Hurtgen Forest back in November of 1944 and had only recently returned to the unit. He was a good soldier and volunteered to be first scout even though as a veteran combat soldier, he knew it was the most dangerous job in the infantry.

On the other side of the road in the woods there were a lot of German vehicles that had been set afire by our artillery. We passed them up and were careful not to touch anything for fear that it might be booby trapped. After we had completely circled the crossroads,

---

[102] Pfc. Claud C. Carter

we came down to the hotel which was located there and started digging in around it to protect the crossroads. I dug myself a fairly good hole for the night near one of the tanks and filled it with straw from the hotel. During the night a German tank, the one that had been around us for the last few days, ran out of gas and its crew came in and surrendered, leaving the tank sitting in the middle of the road.

April 18

The next morning, the battalion once again changed its course. Turning right at the cross roads we started back towards Harzegerode, some ten miles across the mountains. Our platoon was put on the right side of the road going to Harzegerode and a platoon of G company was put on the other side. We walked through the woods and over the mountains clearing them of Germans as we went. It was mighty rough going for awhile, walking through the thick woods with the little scrub pines still wet from the rain the night before. We were wringing wet before we had gone any distance at all.

I had a map of the area and I tried to follow our route as we went. We passed a big tower for forest fire control and then we stopped for a break. We moved out again and this time ran onto a bunch of Germans coming down the road. Behind them came one of our black soldiers. Everyone was asking themselves "where did he come from". We never found out how that man had gotten so far up in front of us and took these prisoners. We assumed he came from F Company.

We kept on going over and through some of the roughest country that most of us had ever seen. After walking another hour, we paused to rest again. We all sprawled out on the ground and about five minutes later the platoon sergeant, who was close to me, jumped up and shouted that there were Jerries coming down the road. We yelled for them to surrender, but they had already passed our first scouts, who hadn't seen them. They put their hands over their heads, but when they got up closer to us, they tried to break and run into the woods. We finally captured them after shooting one.

We went on a little farther and came across a big house sitting close to the woods. Several Germans were captured at this house. We pushed on once again and came across some more Germans. We took them without firing many shots, since we had walked up and surprised them. At last, our platoon was taken out of the woods and put on the road itself. Another platoon was sent over to the side of the road in our place. We were just about pooped after climbing up and down those mountains. It was about an hour later that we came out of the woods and into sight of Harzegerode. We moved back into the town relieving the 60th Infantry Regiment who had been holding the town. It was the same town that we had started from three days before. It was now about three in the afternoon and we had covered ten miles that day and a total of almost twenty five miles of rugged mountain country in three days.

After about one hour of rest in the town, we moved out into the woods on the edge of it and proceeded to dig in with a crew of a 76 mm anti tank gun. There was only one squad of us and we were told that we had to hold down that section of the line while a whole German Army was being squeezed towards us.

That afternoon, a little way from Harzegerode, the last man of Company E to be killed in World War II was shot. The man was from the 3rd Platoon and we only heard about it after the action had happened. He was shot by a burp gun on a German half track and his body had to be left laying where he was shot until reinforcements arrived. He was dead when the platoon finally reached him.

We staked out the perimeters of our defensive area and agreed upon a line beyond which anything that moved would be shot. We had extra machine guns and grenades and enough weapons to stop a small army. We spent a tense night in our holes, but nothing happened during the night. It had been a beautiful night and the next day was also nice and sunny.

April 19

I went down into the gully the next morning and slept there until about 2:30 in the afternoon. At that time Donahue, our acting squad leader, came down and woke me and told me to go back to my hole. He said that a German Army was expected to come our direction and they were expected to be in our area by three o'clock that afternoon. We were on guard for the rest of the afternoon. Later we were told that F Company captured a big part of the remains of the German army in their area. We did capture about seven men later that night when they walked up on us in the dark. All together it was a rowdy night. Since there were only fifteen of us in all, we were a little jumpy because we knew that we would be tremenduously outnumbered, if the Germans did come our way. We fired at every shadow in front of us and the machine gun was continually bursting out. A guy in the anti tank squad threw some grenades at something. We later speculated that it must have been a Russian prisoner who had wandered that way.   Whoever it was, shouted something in a Slavic language and took off. That was the last we heard from him.

Our task force took about thirty five thousand prisoners in that pocket in the Harz mountains. No telling how many more we killed. The Germans always had a high number of men that were killed in action. In our unit, we had people killed almost daily. In this diary I have only mentioned the people killed in my platoon of about 36 people. There were many more casualties in E Company that I have not mentioned. As great as our casualties were, their numbers did not compare with the number of dead Germans that we saw laying everywhere.

April 20

The next afternoon we got on a halftrack with the anti tank crew and went about fourteen miles back through the woods to Ballenstedt, where there was a large Hitler Jugend school. We had good accommodations there. In addition to good accommodations, there was every kind of souvenir laying around that you could imagine. I was not in the mood to pick up souvenirs, they meant nothing to me at the time. I didn't think anyone at home would care about them either. Some of the boys sent home entire German uniforms. There were thousands of uniforms in the school along with just about every thing else the German army used.

While we were at Ballenstadt, several of us went back to the rear for showers and it was at this time that I came as close to being shot as at any other time at the front. This time the showers were set up in a large shower room in a school. I took my shower and had come out to the first dressing room to dry off. A military policeman was undressing and had his pistol in his hand. Someone yelled at him that he shouldn't have a weapon in the crowded shower and dressing room. About that time, the gun went off and the bullet went through his hand. By that time, I was just going through the door into the outer dressing room and the bullet came out the door and hit a man standing in the outer room. How it came through the door without hitting me, I will never know.

April 22

Two days later we had to go out overnight on a road block back into the mountains. That was the last night that we ever spent in the open. However, it was a completely uneventful night at the road block. By now, spring had come to Germany and the apple blossoms made a beautiful sight all along the roads in this area.

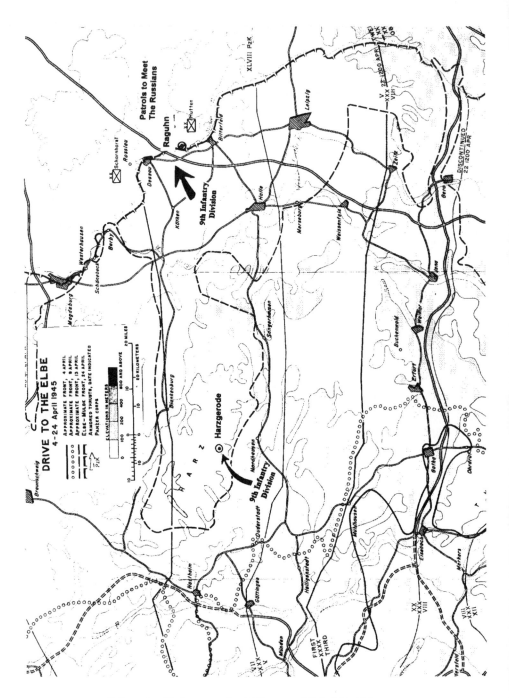

**Map 9 - Drive to the Elbe and Mulde Rivers.
(Final Battle Line of the War)**

Chapter 17

The Fighting Ends
(April 23 through May 9, 1945)

In a few days we left the camp and once again headed towards the fighting which was now along the Elbe River and around the industrial city of Dessau. It took us most of the day to ride the few miles in the cold though the beautiful open country. There was no resemblance to the mountains that we had just left. We passed through several large towns with Kothen being one of them.

We moved into position in small villages and towns along the Mulde River[103]. The small village where we were billeted was named Marke, but it only consisted of a large power plant and some outlying buildings. We stayed in an old wood frame German office building in the area of the power plant and made the best of it. We had a new 2nd Lieutenant in E Company now from West Point. This was the first West Pointer that I had seen below battalion level in my whole career in the military. They must have rushed him up to the front after the fighting was over so that he could say that he had fought in the big war. I have read that this was the case with General Eisenhower's son.

This lieutenant now insisted that we dig foxholes out in the edge of the woods overlooking a wide open area to our front. The ground was sandy, so it was no problem to dig the hole. We dug them just the way that we had always dug them and piled the dirt in a mound around the hole. However, this didn't meet West Point requirements. The lieutenant insisted that we spread the dirt all around so that it would leave no mound around the hole, just the way they taught at

---

[103] The Mulde branches from the Elbe near Dessau and became the demarcation point between the Russians and Americans in this Area

West Point. This was the last foxhole that I ever dug so I am glad that I finally got one right.

The next few days we spent guarding bridges and the nearby power plants. The first day that we got to Marke our artillery was firing over our head; but the next day, the order came down to cease firing and to wait for the Russians. This was the best news that we could have had. We were told that the 9th Division had wound up its fighting days.

On the twenty sixth of April as I was on the way to a movie, Lt. Bonnett, who was then our Battalion S-2 (Intelligence Officer), asked me if I had heard the news, and I told him no. He said that he had gotten news a little while before that Americans had contacted the Russians up at Torgau. We had sent a plane out every half hour from our regiment to keep in touch with the Russians, but as yet we hadn't made any contact with them.

At one o'clock the next afternoon (April 27th) we were alerted for a combat patrol. Before now a combat patrol usually meant lots of trouble and we dreaded them. But today, we all kind of looked forward to this patrol since we thought that we might make contact with the Russians. At about three in the afternoon, we loaded onto half tracks and started out. We crossed through our lines along the Mulde River at Raguhn and from here on we were in enemy territory. However, we rode past long lines of Germans coming in to surrender. Never in my life had I ever seen so many Germans, all in full uniform and well disciplined, coming in to surrender. Along all the roads they were walking or marching toward our lines. We went through several towns as the people lined the streets, waving at us and watching their own army going towards our line. We didn't stop to take prisoners but just waved them on past us. Our objective was to contact the Russians. We must have gone through a half dozen towns and traveled about ten miles into the German lines before we stopped in a town where the 2nd Platoon was taken off the vehicles. We were taken over to a court yard where there must have been a thousand German soldiers gathered together, waiting to be searched and sent back.

We started searching them and taking just about everything they had away from them. The soldiers had bags full of loot that they had been carrying around, and we took all that away from them. We let them keep a lot of their personal gear and most of us didn't bother with picking up any of the loot. I didn't see anything of any real value, and I didn't want to have to carry so much in my pack. Next to the courtyard, there was a place that appeared to be a German military hospital. We couldn't go inside with our weapons according to the *Geneva Convention.* Several of the German officers from the hospital were milling around in the courtyard and one of them was drunk and hysterical. A big black American sergeant walked up to him and knocked him down. One of the high ranking German officers gave the German a tongue lashing and told him that he was a disgrace and did not know how to act as a German officer.

The next thing I knew, they had me and a couple of other fellows in charge of the first group of about one hundred and fifty German prisoners that were to be marched back towards our lines. We started them out down the road and we noticed that there were a bunch of women following the soldiers. After chasing the women off, we finally got our prisoners out of town. But as we were leaving, there were more German soldiers coming in carrying their gear. We just waved them on towards the courtyard. We had about as many prisoners in our column as we could handle.

After we got outside of town we stopped for awhile in a big open field and at about that time Colonel Maness came along and we asked him what we were to do with the prisoners. He told us to stop there and keep them in the field. We did as he said and he left Lt. Bonnett there in charge of them. A few GI trucks came along and we loaded as many as we could onto them. About every few minutes some of the boys in the platoon would bring another batch of about two hundred up to us and put them in the field with our prisoners.

Before we knew it, we had about two thousand prisoners on our hands.

Once during that afternoon, an entire German convoy passed us going towards our line with only one of our tank destroyers driving behind them for a guard. Some of our prisoners that day were policemen from Frankfurt on the Oder and were fleeing from the Russians. We also had policemen from Berlin among the prisoners.

Colonel Maness came back and started questioning the German officers as to where and how many men there were in the vicinity. There was one German who was drunk and acting up and Lt. Bonnett told me to take him out in front of all the rest and make him eat dirt. So I did as he directed and made him lay on the ground with his nose in the dirt until we left there. After that, he didn't cause any more trouble.

There was one jeep that came up with a note from a German prisoner addressed to some fellow. If I remember correctly it went something like this:

Dear Bob,

Well I guess our game is up. The cause is lost now and there is no use for us to think other wise. I suppose our role will be reversed. You will no longer be the prisoner, but now I will be. Good luck.

Your friend,
John

The information that we received at the time was that there were a group of American prisoners that were within a few miles of us and the German officer in charge of them wished to hand them over to us. I don't know what the note was referring to or what happened in regard to the prisoners.

We started back toward our line marching the prisoners ahead of us. I got in one of the half-tracks and rode along in back of them. The line must have stretched for miles down the road. The trucks gradually kept taking the prisoners away until, finally, they were all gone. We got back inside of our own lines at about two in the morning. When we got back to our quarters we were dead tired. What a day it had been. We felt as if the whole German Army had tried to surrender to us. We had hot chow waiting for us and after eating our fill, we finally turned in for a little sleep.

The next day another patrol went out but our platoon didn't go with it. On April 29th, a patrol from the 1st Battalion contacted the Russians at Pratau. That day, we moved into Raguhn on the banks of the Mulde River. On May 4th, a platoon from the 2nd Battalion moved out of Raguhn and immediately contacted the Russians. The Russians arrived on the east bank of the Mulde River across from us a short time later. From that time on, the war was over as far as we were concerned.

While we were in Raguhn, we often went to the Russian side of town and talked to the Russian soldiers. They would show us their weapons and we would show them ours. Everything was on a friendly basis. The Russians would hang big signs out saying "Long may we live in Peace with our great allies the Americans". and other similar things. They came over sometimes and invited us to their dances but the enlisted men were never allowed to go to any of them. Once, while they were visiting, the Russian soldiers said that if we would come visit them they would get girls for us. Then, if they came to America, we could get girls for them. They also said that they were getting ready to help us fight the Japanese.

On Wednesday, May 2, *The Stars and Stripes* announced that Hitler was dead. Soon afterward, a German civilian stopped me on the street and said, "Hitler dead, Roosevelt dead, the war is over, ya". I was disgusted to hear the German say this, but I suppose in the mind of the German civilian, Roosevelt was no better than Hitler, and their combined deaths meant the end of the war.

While we were in Raguhn , we stayed in a large school on the edge of town. It was a very nice building for a barracks and we enjoyed our stay there. During this period, Colonel Ward, the Regimental Commander, broke his ankle and the rumor made the rounds that he fell down the stairs at a Vodka party that the Russians had given. We had no way of verifying that this really happened but it did make a lively story. Never-the-less, life in Raguhn was certainly relaxed during the period that we stayed there. General J. Lawton *"Lightening Joe"* Collins, one of the most famous of all the American Generals, came by one day and spoke to us. He said that he wanted to tell us all good-by before he left the theater. Also, he complimented us on the way the unit had performed in combat. We couldn't get over how young and boyish he looked to be a Lieutenant General[104]. He was quite a striking figure with his blond hair and good looks.

The battalion had already started a training schedule in order to keep us busy and out of trouble. Most of the training consisted of close order drill and calisthenics. Usually we trained in the morning and relaxed in the afternoon. Some days we had inspections. One day during inspection, Col. Maness came around and inspected our rifles. The barrel of my rifle was pitted and he gave me the dickens for this. I had to bite my tongue to keep from telling him how I felt. After all that rifle had gone through, I was surprised it would still fire. Of course, they also threatened to make me pay for the damage I had done when I carved the identifying mark on the rifle stock. Some times you had to wonder if we had fought in the same war.

Some days we were taken over to the Autobahn that went toward Dessau and Berlin. The Autobahn was only about 4 miles from

---

[104] He had been promoted to Lieutenant General on April 16, 1945 and was now supposed to be headed for the Pacific Theater.

Raguhn. Our main job in guarding the Autobahn was to keep the civilians away from it. Everyone in this part of Germany was trying to flee to the west to get away from the Russians. There were also many displaced people from other countries just trying to get back home. We stopped one nice looking woman that supposedly had an order from the American army that would allow her to pass. When we read the official looking letter, we saw that it was signed by General Robert E. Lee, CSA. I suppose that this was a cruel hoax that some GI's had played upon the lady. Maybe they thought that it might get her through if she met the Russians. You couldn't help but feel sorry for some of these people, but most of us had been so hardened by our experiences during the war, that it was difficult to show sympathy toward any of the Germans.

During the early days of May, we kept getting reports over the radio that the Germans were surrendering in Denmark and Italy and various other places. The first notice that we had of the end of the war came from the German radio broadcasts to the German people announcing that Germany had surrendered. I wrote home to say that all of the surrenders didn't really matter much to us because, as far as we were concerned, the war was already over.

VE Day was celebrated on Tuesday, May 8th. We listened to Churchill's speech at 3:00 PM, which more or less formally ended hostilities. Then we went out behind the schoolhouse and fired a German signal pistol into the air. The pistol sounded like a cannon going off and the signal flare burst high in the air and floated slowly to the ground. That was the only celebration that any of us did for VE Day. We didn't see any particular reason to celebrate. None of us expected to be going home anytime soon.

The "Raider" newspaper put out a one page, mimeographed, special edition, dated Tuesday, May 8, 1945, announcing the end of the war and giving details of the surrender. That night, there was a GI show in the theater in downtown Raguhn. We all went to it and thoroughly enjoyed the corny jokes and amateur performances.

May 8th was quite a joyful occasion for the civilians in and around Raguhn. The town was crowded with displaced persons and refugees from all over the eastern part of Germany. Many civilians walked up and down the street past the schoolhouse. I found an old record player and some records of Hitler's speeches and I played these from the balcony over and over again.

The official ceremonies to celebrate the end of the war took place in our battalion on May 9th. It consisted mostly of thanksgiving services where the chaplains gave thanks for our safe deliverance. The chaplain thanked God that we had safely passed through the valley of the shadow of death. This made a strong impression on me. I suddenly realized, that now for the first time, death was not constantly looking over our shoulders. As the chaplain said, we were no longer in the *valley of the shadow of death*. We had lived 24 hours a day fearing for our lives and wondering who would be the next to die. At last, we were safe, for awhile at least.

After the thanksgiving ceremonies, we all posed for pictures. Captain Petty took pictures of the company and we all took pictures of each other. I got together with Denny, one of the fellows from Oklahoma, and we took pictures and had our pictures taken together. Denny and I had gone all the way together from basic training at Camp Wolters to Raguhn Germany. He had been wounded during the time that I was in the hospital and had only recently returned to the company. We had a great time reliving so many of our experiences and talking about the friends that we had known and wondering if they had survived the war. Sergeants Ward and Roberson, my old squad leaders, had both returned to the company here in Raguhn just before the war ended so it was a glorious reunion for those of us that had survived.

That night I wrote home to Lavonne:

.... *"At about ten this morning we had a ceremony to celebrate the end of the war. It was mostly prayers of thanksgiving, thanking the Lord that we were picked to survive this war over here. We also heard a message from the Regimental Commander congratulating us for having such an outstanding record in the war."*.....

"I guess there will be a good many boys coming home now. Some to stay and some just on furlough. I haven't been in long enough to hope for a discharge and I haven't even got enough points to get home.

I guess I had better end this letter for today. Oh yes, there was something the Chaplain said in his prayer today. He thanked God that we had passed through the valley of the shadow of death safely. You can't understand what that means to us. I never really understood what danger was 'til I got into combat, where we were in danger of some kind all of the time. Now, to think that at last we are safe, for awhile at least. Thank God darling for all that he has done for us. I say us, because I know that you shared all of my fears right along beside me. I knew that everything that I did was of some interest to you and I knew that I had someone, or rather a lot of you, who was interested in my safety and whether I got home or not. That helped a lot. I love you more than anything else darling."

The war was definitely, finally, and officially over now. It had been a long hard road across Germany from Belgium and many of our comrades didn't make it. Those of us that made it were just thankful to be alive. But, there was another war in the Pacific, and we couldn't really relax until that one ended.

Epilogue

About a week after the war ended, the 9th Division headed south to Bavaria to take up its position in the Army of Occupation of Germany. The division's fighting days were over, at least for this war. During the fighting in Africa, Sicily and Europe, it had suffered 22,292 casualties, with 4581 of these being killed in action. This was the fourth highest amount of casualties of any unit in the entire army. In the European Theater, the 9th Division was third in the number of battle casualties, following closely behind the 36th and 45th Infantry Divisions that had fought the long bloody war in Italy before entering the action in France and Germany. The 2nd Battalion of the 47th Infantry had received three Distinguished Unit Citations (two citations while I was a member),[105] making it one of the most highly decorated units in the entire army.

After the move to Bavaria, the 9th Division became part of General George Patton's Third Army. The division headquarters was located in Ingolstadt and the 2nd Battalion of the 47th was located in a wooded area near Geiesenfeld, about 10 miles southeast of Ingolstadt. The battalion stayed for only a short time near Geisenfeld. While it was there, it was busy locating permanent billets. Before the end of May these billets had been located in the old monastery town of Scheyern, just a few miles outside of Pfaffenhofen and the battalion moved again.

The 2nd Battalion spent a lazy summer in Scheyern. E Company was located in an old girls dormitory and had the only operating shower facilities in the town. On Wednesday afternoons, the GI's of E Company turned the showers over to the nurses of the MASH unit that was billeted in part of the monastery. Evidently one shower a week was enough for the nurses. The dormitory was a luxury for the

---

[105]Two of the citations were mentioned previously and are included in the appendices. The third citation was for action at Cherbourg in France during June of 1944.

men of E Company, since for the first time they were able to sleep in beds with straw mattresses. This lasted only until lice was discovered on some of the men and all of the mattresses had to be burned.

The men relaxed into the life of a peacetime army but they were still not permitted to fraternize with the German population. Those that violated these rules were placed like animals inside a hastily constructed stockade that was built alongside one of the roads. Most GI's could never understand what the non-fraternization regulations were all about. Were they being protected from being indoctrinated by the German civilians or was it the other way around? By mid-summer, General Eisenhower rescinded the regulation, and life for the GI's returned to a more normal situation.

A ballroom was built in one of the meeting rooms of the monastery, complete with revolving mirrors. The room also served as a movie theater when not being used for dances. Softball games were played every afternoon and a league of teams was organized. USO shows played in the area regularly and, if you were lucky, you could get a ride to one of the major air bases to see Jack Benny, Bob Hope and many other of the big name stars perform.

The 9th Division celebrated its fifth anniversary on August 1, 1945. General Patton came to Ingolstadt to review the men of the division and a gala celebration was held in Ingolstadt, including a performance by Bob Hope and his troop and a boxing demonstration by the heavyweight contender, Billy Conn. Patton reviewed the men of the 9th standing in the back of a staff car, wearing his highly polished helmet, and two pearl handle revolvers. Just to see this legendary figure, sent a thrill through the hearts of the men standing at attention as he passed. Within three months Patton would be dead, but his legend would become even greater after his death.

Many of the old timers had already left the division by August 1. Colonel Maness left the battalion shortly after the move to Scheyern.

Most of the new officers and men that came to the unit were from divisions such as the 56th Infantry Division, which most of 9th Division men had never heard of before. Many of the rest were still awaiting orders to go to the Pacific theater. On August 16th, the day that Victory over Japan was celebrated in the unit, one group of men scheduled to go to the Pacific lined up outside the headquarters at Scheyren. At about 2 PM, word came for the men to stand down, they would not be shipping out. Everyone still left in the unit let out a great sigh of relief. The war was finally over.

Bibliography

Blumenson, Martin. *The Battle of the Generals.* New York, 1993.

Chamberlain, Peter et al., *German Fighting Vehicles 1939-1945.* London 1975

Currey, Cecil B., *Follow Me and Die,* Stein and Day, New York, 1984.

Ellis, Chris et al., *German Tanks 1939-45.* Great Britain, 1975.

Forty, George., *U. S. Army Handbook 1939-1945.* London, 1975.

Gillespie, David E., et al. *History of the 47th Infantry Regiment.* Germany, 1945.

McDonald, Charles B., *The Last Offensive,* Office of Chief of Military History, Washington, D.   C., 1973.

McDonald, Charles B. and Mathews, Sidney T., *Three Battles: Arnaville, Altuzzo, and Schmidt.*   Office of Chief of Military History, Washington,   D. C., 1952.

McDonald, Charles B., *The Siegfried Line Campaign*, Office of Chief of Military History, Washington, D. C., 1963

Mittleman, Joseph B., *Eight Stars to Victory*, Ninth Infantry Division Association, Washington   1948.

Phillips, Henry Gerard, *Remagen, Springboard to Victory,* H.G. Phillips, Penn Valley, Calif, 1995.

Strawson, John, *The Battle For The Ardennes,* B. T. Batsford Ltd., London 1972.

Whiting, Charles, *Bloody Aachen,* Leo Cooper, Ltd., London, 1976.

Whiting, Charles, *Siegfried, The Nazis Last Stand,* Stein & Day, New York, 1982.

About the Author

Private First Class Jack R. Blann left E Company in June of 1945 to work in the communications section of 2nd Battalion Headquarters. In the fall of 1945 he became a battalion clerk and administered the first currency control program instituted in the battalion. Then, in January of 1946 he took over the job of clerk of Headquarters Company, 2nd Battalion. In February of 1946, he was assigned to the 47th Infantry Regiment Headquarters as a staff writer for the regimental newspaper, *The Raider*. He remained on the staff of the newspaper until he returned to the states and was discharged in June of 1946. Jack R. Blann and Lavonne Fischer were married one month after he returned home.

Blann returned to Texas A&M and completed his work towards a degree in Civil Engineering. Immediately after graduating from Texas A&M in 1949, he applied for a direct commission as a Reserve Officer in the Corps of Engineers. In the summer of 1950, he received his commission as a Second Lieutenant in the Corps of Engineers and was called to active duty soon thereafter for the Korean War. He served in Arizona on the staff of an Engineer Aviation Battalion during the Korean War and returned to inactive duty in 1952 without going overseas.

Although employed full time as a staff engineer by Exxon, Blann continued his career in the Army Reserves after leaving active duty. He completed many officer career schools including the Command and General Staff College, where he graduated with honors. He rose in the Army Reserves to the rank of Colonel, which he held at his retirement in 1986. At the completion of his active career in the Army Reserve, Colonel Blann was awarded the Legion of Merit for outstanding service to his country. His other decorations include the

Meritorious Service, the Bronze Star, and the Purple Heart Medals, and the Combat Infantryman's Badge.

Jack and Lavonne Blann now live in Houston, Texas. They have three grown children, one son and two daughters, and seven grandchildren.

E Company Prepares to Advance Into Germany (Signal Corps Photo From National Archives). People are identified from left to right as Shambrock-far left ,unknown - 2nd, Jensen - 3rd, Capt. Petty - 4th , Lt. Kenney 5th and Snider - 6th

Lt. Kenny in the Snow at Kalterherberg

L to R - Lt. Severson, H Co.; Lt. Kenny, E Co.; and Lt. Hill of H. Co.
photographed during the push across Germany. H Company's heavy weapons were
quite often in support of E Company.

Destruction at Vettelschoss.
E Company attacked town from right to left through the woods in the background.

Mace Plays the Guitar at Vettelschoss While Lillifors Reads his Mail.
Church in background was focus of the attack on Vettelschoss for several hours

In this 1978 photo, Oberkirchen appears much as it did in 1945 when Capt. Petty led E Company in the attack across the field in the foreground.

The old woodcutters house on the hill above Oberkirchen where Hamlet and the author sought shelter during the first night of the battle. This photo was taken in 1978. The building has since been removed and replaced with a modern hunting lodge.

During 1978 visit to the Oberkirchen battleground, the author stands in foxhole that he and Hamlet dug on top of hill above the town of Oberkirchen.

171

The Author Prepares to Board a Tank Near Velmede in the Ruhr Pocket

2nd Platoon of E Company Moves Through a Deserted Town in The Ruhr

Hart and Donaho Horse Around With a Flare Pistol.
Note the equipment each carries.   Hart on the left has a BAR with clips for it on his belt and a gas mask pouch at his side. Donaho has two bandoleers of ammunition around his chest and an entrenching tool at his side.

F Company Patrol Returns to Tilkerode After Encountering Tiger Tank

Lt. Col. Maness posses with 2nd Battalion Company Commanders near the end of the fighting. Back row (L to R) - Capt Schmader, F. Co.; Lt. Col. Maness, Bn. Cmdr.; Lt. Kenny, G Co.; and Capt. Compton, Hq. Co.. Front Row (L to R) - Capt. Petty, E Co.; and Capt. Laurenz, H Co.

174

Sergeant W. H. "Hamp" Ward
Squad Leader, 2nd platoon, E Company

PFC. Walter F. McLhinney, Capt. Petty's radioman, killed in action by German panzer
faust at Oberkirchen, Germany, 3 April 1945

L to R - Cook, Blann, and Hart wait for the Russians at Marke in April of 1945

This Photo shows the confusion at the Checkpoint in Raguhn.
Russian Sentry is in the Foreground

Confident Russian sentry talks to crowd outside Russian headquarters in Raguhn.

Sergeant Bill Roberson relaxes with members of 2nd Platoon after VE Day is announced. Riley is the soldier reclining on his arm in the right portion of the picture and Garrard is looking at the camera in the lower right corner

Hart & Donahue Take a Dip in the Mulde River at Raguhn

178

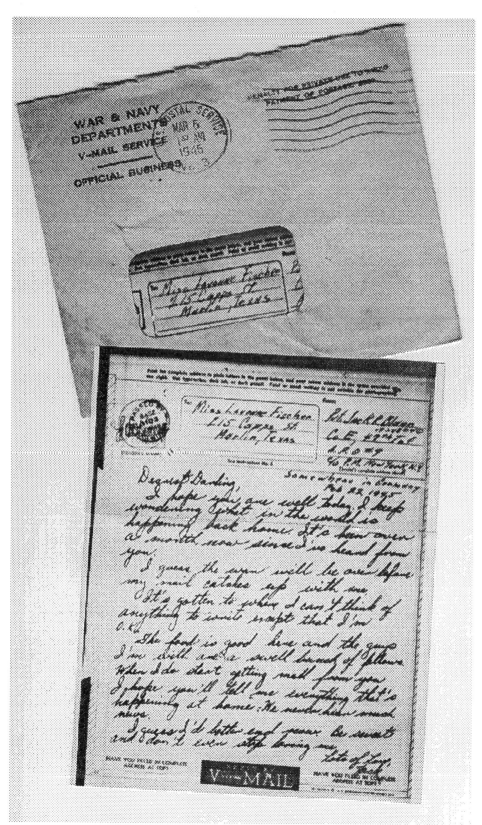

V-Mail Letter From The Front

LIEGE ED

THE STARS A

Daily News paper of U.S. Armed Forces

Vol. I—No. 49

1st ARMY AC

Reds Only 28 Mi. From Berlin—Foe

Powerful Russian attacks against the "outer ramparts" of the Berlin defense system were reported yesterday by German commentators, who said that Marshal Gregory Zhukov's Red Army forces had driven 10 miles west of the Oder River and reached the town of Seelow, only 28 miles from the German capital.

Nazi reports that Zhukov had opened his drive for Berlin still were not officially confirmed by the Russians. But Moscow radio broadcast this message to the people of Berlin: "Your last hour has struck. This is your last chance."

The Russian force which reached Seelow had broken out of the Oder bridgehead opposite Goritz, six miles south of the enemy bastion of Kustrin, the Germans reported. Nazi forces were reported to have retaken some ground in counter-attacks.

Assault Under Way

This and other Nazi accounts of action on the Kustrin-Frankfurt front and above Kustrin indicated that Zhukov's long-awaited assault was well under way. The Germans said that fierce fighting was in progress, with some localities changing hands hourly.

The Russians were reported to have captured Rathstock, west of the Oder on the Kustrin-Frankfurt road, as well as Klessin, in the Oder loop to the southeast. The Germans claimed to have re-entered Rathstock and said that in Klessin "The remnants of the Russian defenders were crushed."

Northwest of Kustrin, the Germans said, Zhukov intensified his attacks near Zehden and plunged forward to Niederwutzen, 31 miles northeast of Berlin.

Hit Near Manschow

Scene of Reported Crossir

Stars and Str

Reuter and BBC reported last night that the First U.S. Army the Rhine was at Remagen. There was no official announcceme Meanwhile, Associated Press reported the Third U. S. Army was from a junction with the First.

TION
ND STRIPES

In the European Theater of Operations

Friday, March 9, 1945

Ici On Parle Français

Il pleuvra demain.
Eel pluvra duh-maa.
It will rain tomorrow.

ROSS RHINE

s Map by Brown
idgehead across
of the location.
s than 25 miles

Forges Bridgehead South of Cologne In Surprise Move

By Dan Regan
Stars and Stripes Staff Writer

FIRST U.S. ARMY HQ., Mar. 8—First Army troops crossed the Rhine south of captured Cologne at 1640 o'clock Wednesday and since then have established a firm bridgehead on the east bank of the river, it was officially announced tonight.

(Late Reuter reports said that "strong forces of infantry are still streaming across the Rhine against disorganized Germans.")

(Location of the crossing was not officially announced. Reuter and BBC both reported that the crossing was made at Remagen, about halfway between Cologne and Coblenz. Earlier, the Nazis asserted that a force of Americans had reached the Rhine at Remagen.)

Apparently hitting the Germans where they least expected such a blow, Gen. Hodges' men hurdled a major obstacle in the Allied drive to the industrial Ruhr in bridging the river.

Temporary News Blackout

(Meanwhile, Associated Press reported from Supreme Allied Headquarters that a temporary news blackout had dropped over the last gap—well under 25 miles— separating the First Army from Gen. Patton's Third U.S. Army spearheads, which reached the Rhine north of Coblenz Wednesday.

(Germans fleeing across the Rhine at Andernach, nine miles northwest of Coblenz, were reportedly being shelled by artillery of Patton's Fourth Armd. Div., which made the sensational 60-mile dash to the river. Remagen is at the junction of the Cologne-Coblenz and Ahr Valley rail lines. The town is on the left bank of the Rhine, about 12 rail miles south of Bonn. The Ludendorf Bridge, a

Nazis Strafe Bridgehead

By Andy Rooney
Stars and Stripes Staff Writer

EAST OF THE RHINE, Mar. 8—Able Co. crossed first, Charlie second and Baker Co. followed them and went on to take the high cliff rising sharply behind the beachhead.

That is the simple story of the American crossing of the Rhine—where they crossed and how they crossed are secrets, although the Germans sent single planes over at intervals, attempting to strafe the American flow across the great Ger-

PARIS EDITION

EXTRA # THE STARS AND STRIPES **EXTRA**

Daily Newspaper of U.S. Armed Forces in the European Theater of Operations

Vol. 1 — No. 285   1 Fr.   1 Fr.   Tuesday, May 8, 1945

VICTORY

Nazis Reveal Surrender To Western Allies, Russia

The unconditional surrender of Germany to the Western Allies and Soviet Russia was announced by the German high command yesterday morning.

The official announcements from the Allied governments are expected to come simultaneously from Washington, London and Moscow today.

The British Ministry of Information, proclaiming that today would be 'Victory in Europe Day,' said Prime Minister Churchill would make 'an official announcement' at 3 PM.

President Truman said he had agreed with the British and Russian governments that no surrender proclamation would be made 'until simultaneous announcements could be made by the three governments.'

King George VI of England sent Gen. Eisenhower a cablegram last night

Nazis Still Fight Reds At Prague

Russian and U.S. Third Army troops, despite Germany's reported unconditional surrender, continued their drive into Czechoslovakia yesterday after the Nazi occupation there announced it would still not war with Reds.

With Prague's future hanging in the balance, way of its opening bowed after and it was still feebly by powers of resistance. A Czech radio report deteriorated yesterday morning

Prayer, Tears, Laughter — The World Celebrates

By David A. Gordon

People in Allied cities throughout the world yesterday accepted the news of the reported unconditional surrender of Germany at face value—despite lack of official announcements from the governments of the U.S., Britain and Russia—and celebrated with prayer, tears and laughter.

It was noted in the speech of the world's great cities—Times Square, New York; Trafalgar Square and Piccadilly Circus in London; and along the Champs Elysees, Paris—that it was a mood to join people in praise of the German Armies vowed to its, the feeling of triumph.

Ticker Tape Showers Wall Street

Here, too, the huge crowds took the word on about Japan, but still far ahead; the restful ring and the shortlived Wall Street the absence of work tickets and telling tape down showed carnivalized exuberance.

Ticker tape poured from the office windows of Wall Street and scraps of garbage spots from the windows of the Customs

congratulating him and his armies on the 'complete and crushing victory' in Europe.

The Associated Press broke the news of the surrender in a story from Rheims, France, that the Allies had announced Germany's surrender at 0241 hours yesterday morning. It said the surrender took place in the little red school house that is Gen. Eisenhower's headquarters.

Col. Gen. Gustaf Jodl, German army chief of staff, signed for Germany, it was reported.

The Associated Press story apparently was premature. Front dispatches coming from Washington to London, it appeared that arrangements were made to announce the surrender simultaneously in the three capitals when the news broke. This seems

GERMANY EDITION
Volume 1, No. 35
Wednesday, May 2, 1945

THE STARS AND STRIPES

Daily Newspaper of U.S. Armed Forces in the European Theater of Operations.

Russian Lesson
Gde nakhoditsya...?
Where are the soldiers?

HITLER DEAD

7th Clears Munich

Yank Armor Across Elbe With British

Munich, capital of Bavaria and home of the Nazi movement, today was completely in the hands of 7th Army troops.

Far to the north, troops of the US 2d Armored Div. linked up with British under Field Marshal Bernard L. Montgomery's command, pushing east from their Elbe River bridgehead in a drive to clear the Baltic coastal plain and seal off Denmark from the greater Reich.

Allied gains along the southern base of the front, from Lake Constance to the junction of the German, Austrian and Czech borders, chipped new areas from the presumed Nazi bastion in the mountains of Central Europe.

Reds Gain on Baltic, Race Into Moravia

MOSCOW, May 1 (Reuter)—Capture of Stralsund, on the Baltic Sea opposite the island naval base of Rugen, was announced tonight in an order of the day from Marshal Stalin.

Marshal Rokossovsky's White Russian Army had also advanced to within 36 miles of Rostock, and Grevesmuhlen, Malchin, Waren and Wesenberg, important communications centers, have fallen.

On the southern front, the Soviet offensive in Czechoslovakia advanced swiftly following capture of Moravska-Ostrava in the north. Collapse of the whole area back to Prague, the Czech capital, was impending.

The battle of Berlin had developed into a dramatic mopping-up operation. Though some German troops were still fighting fanatically, the Nazi defense was broken and many Volkssturm units were laying down their arms, sometimes entire whole streets with white flags.

Against this, however, some SS battalions had made suicide pacts to go down with the buildings they were defending.

Heil-Style Salute Banned for PWs

OMAHA, May 1 (ANS)—German PWs in this country have been forbidden to use the straight-arm Fascist salute. Maj. Gen. C. H. Danielson, commanding general of Seventh Service Command, said a War Department order affecting German and Italian PWs requires that the U.S. salute be used.

He added that all German flags with the swastika would be...

Adolf Hitler died yesterday afternoon, the Germans announced last night.

Declaring that Grand Admiral Karl Doenitz, former commander-in-chief of the German Navy, was Hitler's successor, the radio declared:

"It is reported from Der Fuehrer's headquarters that Der Fuehrer Adolf Hitler has fallen this afternoon at his command post in the Reich Chancellery, fighting to the last breath against Bolshevism and for Germany.

"On April 15, Der Fuehrer appointed Grand Admiral Doenitz as his successor. Our new Fuehrer will speak to the German people."

Then Doenitz, in a radio talk to the German people, said:

"German men and women, soldiers of the German Wehrmacht:

"Our Fuehrer, Adolf Hitler, has fallen. The German people bow in deepest mourning and veneration.

"My first task is to save the German people from destruction by Bolshevism. If only for this task, the struggle will continue."

Bernadotte Denies Second Himmler Bid

STOCKHOLM, May 1 (Reuter)—Count Folke Bernadotte, Swedish intermediary who brought the original offer of Heinrich Himmler, German Gestapo chief, to surrender to the U.S. and Britain, denied today on his return to Sweden that he had seen Himmler on his latest visit to Germany or brought a message back...

Appendix A

Distinguished Unit Citation

The 47th Infantry Regiment with the following attached units:

> 84th Field Artillery Battalion;
> Company B, 9th Medical Battalion;
> Company B, 15th Engineer Battalion;
> Company A, 746th Tank Battalion;
> Company C, 899th Tank Destroyer Battalion;

These units distinguished themselves by extraordinary heroism and outstanding performance of duty in gallantly holding and extending the important Remagen bridgehead over the Rhine River in Germany from 8 to 19 March 1945. The 47th Infantry Regiment, and attached units, were ordered on 7 March 1945 to cross the Ludendorff Bridge over the Rhine, which had been seized intact by elements of the 9th Armored Division. The 2d Battalion, 47th Infantry Regiment, arrived at Remagen early on 8 March and immediately crossed the river. Committed to action at once, it passed through Orsberg and attacked toward Bruchhausen, where all resistance was overcome. The remainder of the regiment moved swiftly across the river during the day. The 1st Battalion seized Scheuren and the 3d Battalion took Ohlenberg, where some of the stiffest resistance in the bridgehead was developed by tanks, self-propelled guns, and well-organized enemy infantry. All battalions were immediately counterattacked, but these savage thrusts by the enemy were smashed after bitter fighting. Committed in the center of the bridgehead, the 47th Infantry Regiment was the first complete infantry regiment to cross the Rhine. It was to maintain its foothold and attack to the east, northeast, and southeast to deepen the vital bridgehead and protect the extremely important Ludendorff crossing. The infuriated enemy, who by this time had recovered from the initial surprise of the crossing, reacted savagely to the thrust of (sic) Germany. On 9 March, the regiment continued the attack eastward against the violent resistance of a determined enemy, amply supported by artillery, tanks, and self-propelled guns. Each gain was subject to numerous counterattacks. Integrated enemy units including the 11th Panzer

Division, were thrown at the bridgehead, and they concentrated much of their power in the center against the *47th Infantry Regiment.* Although constant enemy counterattacks made rest impossible, the regiment slowly but surely cut its way forward over the hilly, wooded terrain. Infantrymen destroyed tanks, captured guns, overran antiaircraft guns, and by 16 March, had forced the enemy out of Notscheid, after bloody house-to-house fighting. Allowing the Germans no time for rest, the regiment continued attacking and took Vettelschoss, building by building, and pressed courageously forward against ever increasing resistance to seize Hohnet. Finally, the autobahn was reached and the initial bridgehead line attained. As the keystone in the arch of the Remagen bridgehead, this gallant force had advanced 12,000 yards in 12 days against great odds. It had pitted its strength, its fortitude, and its bitterly earned combat experience against a desperate, aggressive, and, at times, a numerically superior enemy, and, by cool courage, driving force, and utter disregard for personal safety, had sustained and expanded the Remagen bridgehead on the east side of the Rhine River. The determination and indomitable spirit of the courageous officers and men of the *47th Infantry Regiment*, with attached units, exemplify the finest traditions of the military service.

Appendix B

Distinguished Unit Citation

The 2ND BATTALION, 47TH INFANTRY, reinforced, is cited for conspicuous battle action and outstanding performance of duty during the period of 2 to 5 April 1945. The town of Oberkirchen, Germany, one of the key points in the enemy escape route and so situated that it controlled the road-net so vital to the enemy communications and supply, was assigned as an objective to the 2ND BATTALION (Reinforced) and at 0800 hours, 2 April 1945, the battalion jumped off to seize this objective. Advancing over seven (7) miles of difficult, hilly and exposed terrain. and under intense small arms and mortar fire along the entire route, the battalion, Company "G" leading, passed through Welminghausen and ran Into heavily fortified positions, and after an extremely bitter and aggressive hand to hand fight, cleared the woods with the following results: Thirty (30) enemy dead, eight (8) enemy wounded, and fifty-two (52) captured. The battalion continued onward with supporting machine gun and tank fire from the 2nd platoon. 746th Tank Battalion, though still under intense enemy small arms, and now artillery fire, and entered Vewald, where Company "G", under direct fire from three (3) Mark IV Tanks and artillery, drove the enemy from the town, and caused the tanks to withdraw, after a hand to hand, house to house, struggle, which caused the enemy the following casualties: Ten (10) enemy dead and forty (40) captured. The advance which now came under heavy artillery and self-propelled gun fire, continued to the objective. where, after on intense artillery barrage, Companies "E" and. "F" advanced over exposed terrain which was under deadly small arms, mortar, artillery, sell-propelled. and point blank fire, from five (5) enemy tanks, entered the town at 1500 hours, and by 1830 hours had completely cleared the town of enemy after a bloody hand to hand encounter. An enemy counterattack composed of two hundred (200) infantrymen and six (6) tanks was launched at 1900 hours, which overran part of Company "E" and penetrated two-thirds (2/3) through town. Isolating two (2) platoons of Company "E". At this point the battalion called for, and received, all available artillery fire from the 84th Field Artillery Battalion and Cannon Company, 47th Infantry, on Its own positions. which inflicted many casualties upon the enemy. Company "F" then launched a vigorous attack which succeeded in making contact with Company "E". The lines become fluid, with enemy remaining In scattered groups in the town. Preparations were made for expected counterattacks, including the laying of mines by the 1st Platoon, Company '"B", 15th Engineer Battalion. At 0630 hours the following morning, the enemy launched another attack consisting of two hundred (200) infantrymen and five (5) tanks, in a last desperate effort to drive the battalion from the town. Three platoons were overrun in this attack and enemy tanks penetrated to the center of town. Bazooka teams destroyed three (3) of the enemy tanks from a range of twenty (20) yards and Tank Destroyer fire from the 2nd platoon, 899th Tank Destroyer Battalion, accounted for one (1) more. Fierce and vicious hand to hand fighting and the extreme aggressiveness of the men of the battalion caused the enemy to withdraw in wild disorder. leaving seventy-sight (78) captured and many wounded, and the town safely in hand. During the period 2 to 5 April 1945, the 2ND BATTALION, (Reinforced), 47TH INFANTRY, assaulted and captured three (3) towns, took two hundred and seventy (270) prisoners and hundreds of small arms and automatic weapons, destroyed four (4) enemy tanks, completely annihilated one battalion of infantry and elements of two other battalions. During this period, the battalion operated without flank protection on either flank, suffered numerous casualties which were evacuated by Company "B", 9th Medical Battalion, and crossed more than thirteen (13) miles of heavily defended and difficult terrain, engaged and annihilated a fanatical stubborn enemy by a magnificent display of gallantry, courage and devotion to duty.

Index

185

—F—

F Company, 26, 73, 79, 106, 122, 123, 124, 140, 144, 146
father, R. A. Blann, 7
Fifth Infantry Division, 130
Finnegan, 128
First Army, 17, 35, 54, 56, 71, 72, 84, 90, 97
First Canadian, 33
First French, 33
First Squad, 63
Fischer, Lavonne, 9 , 59, 80, 81, 83, 99, 156
flak, 32
Fort Meade, 17
Forty, George.,, 163
fox-hole, 75, 106
foxhole, 74, 112, 150
France, 19, 20, 25, 26, 48, 111, 124, 159
Frankfurt on the Oder, 152
Frauenberg, 62
French people, 121
Fronhausen, 97
fur lined foxhole, 112

—G—

G Company, 41, 42, 45, 46, 64, 73, 76, 100, 140
Garner, Lt. Jay, 26
Gartenhaus of Falkenberg, 143
Gearhart, 49
Geich, 45, 46, 50, 62
Geiesenfeld, 159
General Milliken, Commander of the III Corps, 72. *See* Milliken
General Van Fleets III Corps, 91
Geneva Convention, 151
German ammo dump, 102
German buzz bombs, 53
German defensive position, 120
German Eleventh SS Panzer Army, 134
German invasion of Norway, 9
German invasion of Poland, 8

German prisoners, 49, 52, 67, 102, 139, 151
German SS troops, 134
German V1 rocket, 53
German V1 rockets, 53
Germany, 17, 21, 22, 23, 32, 33, 35, 64, 72, 84, 90, 97, 98, 111, 121, 131, 147, 155, 156, 157, 159, 163
Gestapo, 97
Gerrard, 61
Gevlinghausen, 117
GI's, 35, 40, 42, 86, 93, 101, 155, 159, 160
Gillespie, David E.,, 163

Girkhausen, 99
Grave Registration Units, 37

—H—

H Company, 109, 114, 123
Hamlet, 108, 109, 112, 115
Harscheidt,, 25
Hart, PFC Howard, 27, 34, 45, 60, 61, 62, 63, 64, 68, 74, 75, 76, 79, 80, 116, 119, 121, 122, 125
Harz mountain, 131
Harzgerode, 133, 137, 143
heavy mortars, 107, 111
heavy weapons, 23, 24, 48, 107, 109, 111
Helborn, 93
Hell on Wheels, 89
Henry Aldrich Show, 18
Hermerzheim, 62
Hitler, Adolph, 8, 21, 57, 137, 147, 153, 156
Hodges, Lt. Gen. Courtney H., 33, 59, 72
Holy Roman Empire, 22
Hope, Bob, 160
Horbeck, 139, 140
Hudson River, 19
Hurtgen Forest, 21, 143